T0273955

Business Analysis for Practitioners: A Practice Guide

Second Edition

Library of Congress Cataloging-in-Publication Data

Names: Project Management Institute.
Title: Business analysis for practitioners : a practice guide.
Description: Second edition. | Newtown Square, Pennsylvania : Project
   Management Institute, [2023] | Summary: "Business Analysis for
   Practitioners: A Practice Guide - Second Edition makes business analysis
   accessible in your professional and daily life, helping you apply
   business analysis skills to solve problems. You'll learn the context,
   environment, and practice of business analysis that can lead to
   successful outcomes. Use this guide to embrace a business analysis
   mindset for successful investigation and discovery-and as a tool to
   achieve outcomes. Adopting this mindset can help you develop an openness
   to questioning, learning, and solution options that are the core of
   business analysis work. The guide can also assist you in developing a
   free and open flow of communication and ideas, creating a platform for
   organizational prosperity. This rich publication provides a sound basis
   for business analysis to deliver a positive impact on your project
   success rates"-- Provided by publisher.
Identifiers: LCCN 2023042394 (print) | LCCN 2023042395 (ebook) | ISBN
   9781628258080 (paperback) | ISBN 9781628258097 (ebook)
Subjects: LCSH: Project management. | Business planning. | Management.
Classification: LCC HD69.P75 B8745 2023 (print) | LCC HD69.P75 (ebook) |
   DDC 658.4/04--dc23/eng/20231023
LC record available at https://lccn.loc.gov/2023042394
LC ebook record available at https://lccn.loc.gov/2023042395

ISBN: 978-1-62825-808-0

Published by: Project Management Institute, Inc.
                   18 Campus Blvd., Ste. 150
                   Newtown Square, Pennsylvania 19073-3299 USA
                   PMI.org
                   Phone: +1 610 356 4600

To place an order or for pricing information, please contact Independent Publishers Group:

Independent Publishers Group
Order Department
814 North Franklin Street
Chicago, IL 60610 USA
Phone: 800 888 4741
Fax: +1 312 337 5985
Email: orders@ipgbook.com (For orders only)

10 9 8 7 6 5 4 3 2 1

Notice

The Project Management Institute, Inc. (PMI) standards and guideline publications, of which the document contained herein is one, are developed through a voluntary consensus standards development process. This process brings together volunteers and/or seeks out the views of persons who have an interest in the topic covered by this publication. While PMI administers the process and establishes rules to promote fairness in the development of consensus, it does not write the document and it does not independently test, evaluate, or verify the accuracy or completeness of any information or the soundness of any judgments contained in its standards and guideline publications.

PMI disclaims liability for any personal injury, property or other damages of any nature whatsoever, whether special, indirect, consequential or compensatory, directly or indirectly resulting from the publication, use of application, or reliance on this document. PMI disclaims and makes no guaranty or warranty, expressed or implied, as to the accuracy or completeness of any information published herein, and disclaims and makes no warranty that the information in this document will fulfill any of your particular purposes or needs. PMI does not undertake to guarantee the performance of any individual manufacturer or seller's products or services by virtue of this standard or guide.

In publishing and making this document available, PMI is not undertaking to render professional or other services for or on behalf of any person or entity, nor is PMI undertaking to perform any duty owed by any person or entity to someone else. Anyone using this document should rely on his or her own independent judgment or, as appropriate, seek the advice of a competent professional in determining the exercise of reasonable care in any given circumstances. Information and other standards on the topic covered by this publication may be available from other sources, which the user may wish to consult for additional views or information not covered by this publication.

PMI has no power, nor does it undertake to police or enforce compliance with the contents of this document. PMI does not certify, test, or inspect products, designs, or installations for safety or health purposes. Any certification or other statement of compliance with any health or safety-related information in this document shall not be attributable to PMI and is solely the responsibility of the certifier or maker of the statement.

Table of Contents

List of Figures and Tables

Figures

Tables

Introduction

This practice guide describes business analysis domains, long-established and current business analysis practices and techniques, and the characteristics of the business analysis mindset, incorporating them into a case study to illustrate ways to use them. The business analysis practices in this guide may be used by practitioners of all types to drive successful outcomes in any type of organization or initiative.

How This Practice Guide Is Organized

This practice guide is organized into five domains with three key practices in each domain. Each practice includes an explanation of what it entails, why it is important, and a case study to illustrate ways to use it. The inclusion of these particular practices reflects their value and applicability in organizations using any approach, whether predictive, adaptive, or hybrid. The sequence in which they are presented is logical (for example, it's hard to refine a solution until a solution exists); however, it is not intended to suggest a fixed order.

While the domains are inclusive of the overall discipline of business analysis, the three practices included within each domain are the most essential practices, as opposed to an exhaustive inventory of practices. A brief statement in a blue-shaded box is featured at the beginning of each practice to express how the business analysis practitioner's mindset impacts the business analysis activities described in that practice.

A case study accompanies the description of each practice to give the reader an idea of its value and how the practice may be applied. The tools used in the case study are a sample from the inventory of tools business analysis practitioners may use. Other tools may be applied, however, some of which could be applied in different ways, based on the initiative.

The case study includes two solutions, each within a different initiative and type of approach. While one project uses a predictive approach and the other an adaptive approach, they are not strictly predictive or adaptive. The intent of the case study is to highlight the pragmatism of good business analysis by illustrating how business analysis practitioners, through different approaches, can use the tools that work best for them and still collaborate effectively to meet the business need. The aim is that business analysis practitioners see similarities to their own environments, which are often blended or hybrid.

The five domains and three practices within each domain are outlined below.

Business Value Assessment

Business Value Assessment includes practices to analyze the situation, assess the current internal and external environment, and evaluate existing organizational capabilities to identify gaps between the current and future states, and propose solutions that add business value and meet business needs. The three practices in this domain are:

- Understand the Situation
- Find the Gaps
- Define the Solution

Business Analysis Planning

Business Analysis Planning includes the practices to ensure an optimal method is used for the business analysis work to be done given the stakeholders' characteristics, needs, organizational context, and approach to be used for the initiative. The three practices in this domain are:

- Understand Business Analysis Governance

- Determine Stakeholder Engagement Approach

- Plan Business Analysis Work

Solution Refinement

Solution Refinement includes the practices related to partnering with stakeholders to elicit requirements and other solution information to iteratively refine the solution once it is initially defined in the business value assessment. The three practices in this domain are:

- Elicit Solution Information

- Analyze Solution Information

- Package Solution Information

Organizational Transition and Solution Evaluation

Organizational Transition and Solution Evaluation covers the transition between the end of solution development and solution implementation, as well as the practice of determining how well an implemented solution, or part of an implemented solution, meets the business value proposition, as articulated in the business case. The three practices in this domain are:

- Enable Organizational Transition

- Facilitate Go/No-Go Decision

- Evaluate Solution Performance

Business Analysis Stewardship

Business Analysis Stewardship includes the practices of ensuring that business analysis activities, artifacts, and deliverables are of high value and that practitioners are mindful of their ethical obligations to stakeholders, the organization, and the environment when doing business analysis work. The three practices in this domain are:

- Promote Business Analysis Effectiveness

- Enhance Business Analysis Capability

- Lead Business Analysis with Integrity

Common Vocabulary

This section provides a few definitions of terms used in this document. See the glossary or visit PMIstandards+® via the QR code to the right or https://standardsplus.pmi.org/ for additional terms not defined below.

Business Analysis

Business analysis encompasses the value-oriented approaches, practices, disciplines, and mindsets that guide the identification of organizational needs; recommendation of potential solutions, elicitation, communication, and management of requirements; facilitation of successful solution implementation; and evaluation of the solution.

Tactically, business analysis is the application of knowledge, skills, tools, and techniques to:

- Determine problems and opportunities;

- Identify business needs and recommend viable solutions to meet those needs and support strategic decision-making;

- Elicit, analyze, specify, communicate, and manage requirements and other solution information; and

- Define benefits and approaches for measuring and realizing value and analyzing the results once solutions are implemented.

Solution

A solution is something that is produced to deliver measurable business value to meet the business need and expectations of stakeholders. It may be produced by a portfolio component, program, or project. A solution could be one or more new products, components of products, or enhancements or corrections to a product. Solutions may include technology, processes, people, and anything else included in the value delivered to meet the business need.

Product

A product (also referred to as a material or good) is an artifact that is produced, is quantifiable, and can be either an end item in itself or a component item. Products are created or updated as parts of solutions to address business needs; therefore, they provide business value.

Requirements

The PMI Guide to Business Analysis [1][1] defines a *requirement* as "a condition or capability that is necessary to be present in a product, service, or result to satisfy a business need." Requirements and other solution information, such as assumptions, dependencies, constraints, issues, and risks, may be captured in a variety of ways, such as user stories or elements of user stories. They may also be captured more formally in a requirements document, requirements traceability matrix (RTM), or in

---

[1] The numbers in brackets refer to the list of references at the end of this practice guide.

whatever format is of value to the team and stakeholders. When the approach to requirements is more traditional and formal, such as in predictive environments, requirements are often categorized by type:

- **Business requirements.** Describe the higher-level needs of the organization, such as business issues or opportunities, reasons why a project has been undertaken, and measurable goals the business is seeking to achieve. Business requirements provide context for other requirements and the solution to ensure that the result addresses the business need.

- **Stakeholder requirements.** Describe the needs of a stakeholder or stakeholder group, where the term *stakeholder* is used broadly to reflect the role of anyone with an interest in the outcome of an initiative and could include customers, suppliers, and partners, as well as internal business roles. Stakeholder requirements must be met to achieve the business requirements.

- **Solution requirements.** Describe the features, functions, and characteristics of the product, service, or result that will meet the business and stakeholder requirements. Solution requirements are grouped into functional and nonfunctional requirements:

  o **Functional requirements.** Describe the behaviors of the product and include actions, processes, and interactions that the product should perform.

  o **Nonfunctional requirements.** Describe the environmental conditions or qualities required for the product to be effective. A few examples include reliability, security, performance, data retention, availability, and scalability.

- **Transition requirements.** Describe temporary capabilities, such as data conversion and training requirements, and operational changes needed to transition from the current (as-is) state to the future (to-be) state. Once the transition to the future state is complete, the transition requirements are no longer needed.

Other types of requirements include project and quality. Those are typically the responsibilities of the project manager and are not discussed in this guide.

Goals

This edition of *Business Analysis for Practitioners: A Practice Guide* is based on the three goals described below.

Goal #1—Business Analysis Is for Everyone

The first goal of this revision is to communicate an understanding of business analysis in such a way that everyone, regardless of title or role, recognizes that business analysis is part of the work they do. It is needed and used throughout any organization—in the people or human resources department, in finance, in logistics, and in every department of the company. In fact, not only does business analysis happen in business organizations, it occurs everywhere—for example, in community groups, nonprofit groups, nongovernmental organizations (NGOs), schools, and even homes. See Table 1-1 for a description of what business analysis is and what it is not.

Business analysis is what enables anyone to meet the needs of their business, customers, followers, fans, or family. It is what people do to be successful in their roles. People such as:

- *Corporate process owners,* who define processes to meet an emerging business need;

- *Doctors,* who identify the right therapies for patients, given various health factors;

Table 1-1. What Business Analysis Is and What It Is Not

Business Analysis is ...	Business Analysis is not ...
A discipline to be applied at any time and continuously.	A discipline to be applied temporarily at one specific point in time.
Something everyone needs in every position and uses in everyday life.	A skill set unique to a specific group of people called business analysts.
A set of practices and techniques that can apply and add value to every industry.	Only applicable to IT and the software industry.
A set of common practices that can be done by many people collaboratively and iteratively.	A mysterious set of practices done in isolation that only a few technical people know how to use.
Tailored to the organization and stakeholders' needs.	A one-size-fits-all approach that can be applied uniformly across all organizations and industries.

- *Local business owners,* who determine which products or services to provide to meet their customers' needs;

- *Social media influencers,* who strategize what to post and when to garner the most attention and followers;

- *Teachers*, who identify learning needs and develop curricula to fill the knowledge gaps of their students;

- *Coaches*, who analyze the strengths and weaknesses of their players and the competition to develop playbooks and fill team gaps with the right talent; and

- *First responders,* who analyze the context and needs of their communities to develop appropriate responses to crisis situations.

To be sure, practitioners in professional environments are the likely readers of this practice guide. Nevertheless, the goal is to ensure that *everyone* reading this practice guide recognizes that each time they seek to understand the problems and opportunities before them and how best to respond, they are doing business analysis.

Goal #2—Appeal to the Modern Learner

The second goal is to provide a practice guide that appeals to the modern learner, who is likely to avail themselves of social media and other online resources in addition to documents like this practice guide, to quickly find what they need to learn to help improve their business analysis work.

With that in mind, brevity has been an objective during development of this practice guide. The intention is to present highlighted examples of important ideas, recognizing that attempts to cover them all will fall short and that a concise presentation may appeal more to modern learners.

In addition, it is through storytelling that business analysis is made most accessible. The narrative of how practices are applied enables practitioners to recognize what they can do to improve their performance. It is hoped that the stories told in this practice guide give readers a sense of what business analysis is and inspire them to explore further.

After reading this practice guide, next steps could involve a practitioner reaching out to others, doing online searches and experiments, and getting creative with the techniques, ideas, and concepts presented herein. This practice guide is scaled and presented in a way to appeal to modern learners, so they can explore what business analysis is, recognize themselves as business analysis practitioners, and move forward on their own to learn more. When people are confident about applying their inner business analysis practitioner, good things will come to projects, organizations, and personal initiatives.

Goal #3—Embrace a Business Analysis Mindset

The third goal is to frame business analysis in a way that makes it easy to understand and accessible to all types of organizations and practitioners. To that end, this practice guide asserts that:

- *Business analysis is more than a set of practices, a discipline, or a profession.*

- *Business analysis is a mindset that guides transformation capability and serves as a fundamental component of value creation.*

This essential frame of mind that enables anyone doing business analysis work to be effective is characterized by the following:

- **Thinking holistically and systemically.** Business analysis is just that—analysis, which means getting a 360-degree view of a need and solution within organizational, business, market, economic, or other contexts. The business analysis mindset seeks to identify the interdependencies of processes, systems, and functions and the perspectives of those who utilize and own them. The ability to think systemically and see the "big picture" is a key enabler of analytical thinking that helps business analysis practitioners identify interconnectedness within the organization and facilitate analysis from all angles of problems, opportunities, and solutions.

- **Sticking to the need before solutioning.** Effective business analysis requires achieving consensus about the need before considering solutions. This can present challenges when the stakeholders already have solutions in mind before the business analysis practitioner becomes involved. It is a business analysis mindset that inspires the business analysis practitioner to keep asking "why" and to inspire curiosity among stakeholders to obtain buy-in to dig deeper. Courage and tenacity enable the business analysis practitioner to keep stakeholders focused on the need before rushing to solutions.

- **Being an organizational detective.** In the haste to get things done, it is tempting to accept the first answer to questions asked. Information from a single source may be biased and provide an incomplete understanding of a need or solution. Elicited information may also be obtained from people who are unsure about what they know or don't know, but are happy to provide answers to questions anyway. It is incumbent upon business analysis practitioners to ensure that the requirements and solutions are aligned, correct, complete, and valuable by confirming business analysis information with multiple sources. A healthy skepticism enables an effective business analysis practitioner to confidently pursue the confirmation of information.

- **Tailoring stakeholder communication.** Good business analysis drives stakeholder understanding through tailored communication that appeals to different stakeholder styles. The business analysis practitioner communicates visually using models, auditorily in formal or informal discussions, and kinesthetically with collaborative exercises to achieve shared understanding and move the initiative forward. Empathy and listening skills enable business analysis practitioners to develop effective partnerships with all types of stakeholders by communicating in ways that resonate with them.

- **Exploring your inner business analyst.** Business analysis is everywhere and performed by nearly everyone. Some practitioners are professionals with experience and highly developed skills. Others are just discovering their business analysis skills. Embrace it! Be intentional and confident in practicing business analysis. Effective business analysis is both art and science, so try different tools and techniques. A successful strategy in one business unit or organization will not necessarily yield success in a different business unit or organization. There is more than one way to be "right." Creativity and courage enable effective business analysis practitioners to explore different approaches to business analysis in their environment and lead others to try new ways of understanding and meeting business needs. #YouDoBA

The business analysis mindset is at the core of all business analysis practices, as illustrated in Figure 1-1. All business analysis domains and practices are enabled by the business analysis mindset.

Figure 1-1. Business Analysis Practitioner Framework

Business Analysis Value Proposition

Research about the value of business analysis consistently supports the premise that developing business analysis skills and knowledge and using a business analysis mindset is time well spent. Organizations with highly mature business analysis practices demonstrate that business analysis has a tangible impact on their organization's success and provides a competitive advantage. A significantly larger percentage of organizations with a high level of business analysis maturity rank themselves well above average against their peer organizations with regard to key indicators [2].

Delivery of value will be limited as long as people think business analysis is about specific people with a complex set of tools who "gather" requirements. The mission of this revision starts with people seeing themselves in the story of business analysis that is happening everywhere around them and appreciating how accessible and easy it is to learn how to use the tools. When that happens for people working in an office, at home, or anywhere else, the value of their initiatives and the work they do will be magnified.

Long-time practitioners and advocates for business analysis will hopefully find this practice guide and the goals behind its creation to be validating. Those new to business analysis will hopefully be inspired to become a part of the community of practitioners of all types who use a business analysis mindset to maximize the value of the work they do. Everyone can partner to apply the business analysis mindset that makes the business analysis experience more effective and satisfying. By bringing this mindset to their efforts, practitioners will more easily collaborate, be better problem solvers, facilitate change management, promote agility, and more effectively capitalize on the opportunities before them.

How Business Analysis Is Evolving

Although the essential goals of business analysis practices have remained relatively stable over the years, the contexts within which they are performed are perpetually in flux. Business analysis practices have transformed from their origin, when predictive approaches were the norm, through the changes brought on by adaptive approaches, to the virtualization of the tools being used and the geographic distribution of the people using them. Practices went from a step-by-step approach of building document-based requirements to a stewardship role of collaborating with stakeholders to meet the business need and deliver value. The following are a few of the drivers of change that are encouraging the evolution of business analysis practices.

- **Customer centricity.** Business analysis practitioners only do business analysis work when it is of value to people directly or when people act as proxies for the interests of other living beings in the environment. The people whom strategic organizations have foremost in mind are their customers, whether internal or external consumers of a solution. Customer centricity is a business strategy that is predicated on putting the customer first and making decisions based on what is important and of value to them.

  Business analysis practitioners use customer centricity to maintain focus on the value proposition of proposed solutions as defined by the needs of the customer. A compelling product vision, for example, can serve to inspire the team and stakeholders to know what they are doing and why, by highlighting how the solution will benefit the customer. Business analysis practitioners have a multitude of stakeholders to consider and activities to execute. Customer centricity hones their attention and effort on the stakeholders and activities that have the most positive impact on the customer experience.

- **Agility in dynamic business environments.** The case for using adaptive approaches, such as agile, to effectively respond to change and uncertainty continues to resonate with organizations of all types, and the continued adoption of adaptive approaches is providing ample opportunities for business analysis practitioners. The application of business analysis practices in an agile environment is facilitated by the fact that much of what happens in those environments is business analysis. For example, product visioning, product backlog refinement, defining requirements in the form of user stories and acceptance criteria, facilitating solution acceptance, and other activities are fundamentally business analysis activities. Further, traditional business analysis activities related to business rules analysis, nonfunctional requirements definition, and traceability are still needed in an adaptive environment, although they will likely be lighter, less formal, and the results will probably look different. Whether as a team member, proxy product owner, or product owner, agile environments are a natural fit for the skills, tools, practices, and mindset of business analysis practitioners who are product-focused and customer-centric.

- **Need for experienced practitioners.** Experienced business analysis practitioners are in higher demand than ever before [3,4], with opportunities to apply themselves on initiatives that go beyond simple problem-solving or opportunity-capitalizing. Digital transformation and business model changes are common enterprise-level initiatives that demand the most experienced and highest performing business analysis practitioners. Becoming a data-driven organization requires an understanding of not only the technology needed but also the requisite changes in organizational processes and behaviors. This includes new ways of thinking, new ways of interacting with customers and one another, and new skills development across the organization. The doors are wide open for business analysis practitioners to engage at the most strategic levels of the organization—if they have the skills and interest to do so.

- **New technologies, advanced solutions.** The technical elements of many solutions to current business needs are unprecedented in their complexity, both technically and ethically. For example, artificial intelligence (AI) and machine learning (ML) have consequences that are far-reaching and ethically challenging. These and other cutting-edge technologies can compromise individual and organizational privacy, infringe upon intellectual property, and change the lives of stakeholders in ways that are not always predictable.

  The benefit of these rapidly emerging technologies is equally compelling. They can increase productivity at rates previously unheard of and yield insights into customer needs and preferences with a degree of accuracy not previously possible. When applied to processes like data-driven decision-making and design thinking, the result is delivery of a customer experience that customer-centric organizations seek to provide, resulting in better business outcomes.

  Given the work of business analysis, including exploring business needs, developing business cases, eliciting solution requirements, and facilitating solution implementations, business analysis practitioners are in a unique position to understand the impact of these changes to organizations and the people in them. It is incumbent upon practitioners to stay informed of these technologies to keep stakeholders aware of them so risks are mitigated, technologies are ethically utilized, and the significant benefits they provide are captured.

- **Virtual business analysis.** Practitioners have used virtual communication and workspaces before, but working virtually has become the norm for many since the COVID-19 pandemic. Even as the pandemic shifts, it is likely that virtual work environments will remain the preferred method of work for many professionals across many disciplines, including business analysis. For example, before the pandemic, only 6% of the U.S. workforce worked primarily remotely [5].

Now, 22% of professionals are expected to work remotely by the end of 2025 [6]. Other data indicate similar trends in other countries. The shift from face-to-face communication to virtual communication is a major challenge. Unlike face-to-face meetings, in virtual interviews and workshops, business analysis practitioners cannot read body language or perceive eye contact and facial expressions to determine if participants are present, nor can they prevent participants from multitasking, which takes their full attention away from the meeting itself.

Effective business analysis practitioners continue to develop skills, tools, and techniques for working in a virtual environment to conduct workshops and interviews, lead business analysis teams and others, create a positive business analysis culture, and engage stakeholders. For example, various digital environments and platforms have been developed to promote visual collaboration and help all team members connect, collaborate, and create—together. The good news is that these new tools are as easily adopted as discarded, and stakeholders are more rapidly engaged in virtual collaboration than ever before.

2

Business Value Assessment Domain

Introduction

The Business Value Assessment domain consists of business analysis work that is conducted to study a current business problem or opportunity. It looks at the current internal and external environments and capabilities of an organization to determine any gaps in business performance and the ability to meet customer needs and propose viable solution options that, when pursued, would produce value satisfying the business needs of the organization.

What to Expect in This Domain

This section of the practice guide provides an approach to assessing business needs and business value and identifying high-level solutions to address them. Business value assessment includes three key practices that enable the business analysis practitioner to empower the organization and decision makers to ensure that new solutions proposed are aligned with the organizational strategy and portfolio and program objectives and will deliver the intended business value.

- **Understand the Situation** provides ways to think about, learn about, discover, and articulate business problems and opportunities. It answers why we need to initiate a project, program, or portfolio in response to a situation.

- **Find the Gaps** is conducted to assess the internal and external environment and analyze and compare the actual performance and current capabilities of the organization with the expected or desired performance and capabilities. This will help determine how to bridge the gap between the current and desired state of the organization.

- **Define the Solution** enables the business analysis practitioner to assemble the results of the analysis in a way that provides relevant information for decision makers to decide whether an investment in the proposed solution is viable and feasible.

Main Benefits of the Practices in This Domain

Simply put, a business value assessment guides the investment decisions made by organizations. During portfolio and program management, through the practices in this domain and analysis of results, the organization ensures that:

- The performance of a portfolio or program continues to provide expected business value;

- New initiatives align with organizational strategy and the portfolio and program goals and objectives;

- Proposed portfolio components, programs, and projects are well vetted and scrutinized with accurate information; and

- All aspects of a proposed solution are analyzed for value, disbenefits, interdependencies, and risks.

To accomplish this, a business analysis practitioner conducts a business value assessment to help an organization understand a business problem or opportunity in greater detail and make sure the right problem is being addressed.

When a formal assessment is sidestepped, the resulting solution often fails to address the underlying business problem or opportunity—or it provides a solution that is not needed or contains unnecessary features.

Key Questions Answered in This Domain

- What needs to be done to understand the business problem or opportunity?

- What is a situation statement, how is it created, and why is it important?

- How are business needs identified and the business value defined?

- Will the business value satisfy the business need and be aligned with organizational strategy?

- How is the current state assessed and the future state determined?

- What is included in a business case and what are the steps for creating one?

Understand the Situation

```
The business analysis practitioner using a business analysis mindset
strives to understand the situation from different perspectives, detects
clues related to the problem or opportunity, asks a lot of questions,
digs into situations, looks for explanations, and refrains from jumping
to solutions.
```

Overview

An important part of a business value assessment is understanding the situation by identifying problems to be solved or opportunities to be embraced. In this context, the situation is a neutral term that describes the context of the problem or opportunity under consideration.

To ensure a common understanding of the problem or opportunity among the stakeholders, the business analysis practitioner presents the situation in a way that makes sense to all related stakeholders and leads to agreement.

Achieving a shared understanding of the situation is a key concept in assessing business value and also plays a very important role in the rest of the business analysis work, even in portfolio, program, and project management.

While a shared understanding does not need to be formal or complex, it does need to be accurate. If it is not accurate, it does not matter how well the other business analysis activities are done. A solid, well-understood situation description for which there is consensus among stakeholders helps ensure that the organization is headed in the right direction. As a result, business analysis efforts will add value when they address the right problem or opportunity.

Value of Understanding the Situation

To avoid focusing on the solution too soon, the practice of Understand the Situation first tries to analyze the current environment and find out the information that was uncovered by investigating the situation. From there, the business analysis practitioner outlines the "why" for solving a problem or taking advantage of an opportunity using a variety of methods.

Understanding and communicating the "why" helps stakeholders develop a deeper understanding of the business need and value proposition. If the situation is not thoroughly understood, the organization may pursue a solution that neither meets the business need nor generates the intended business value. Successfully articulating an organization's "why" is an effective way to communicate with employees, customers, and other stakeholders of the organization; define its particular value proposition; and inspire them to take action.

According to Sinek's Golden Circle theory [7], many people think from the outside in—what » how » why. People know "what" they want to deliver and some of them know "how" they're going to deliver it, but most people do not focus on the "why." The research found that only 24% of companies explicitly express their "why" compared to the "how" and "what" results.

While understanding the situation, a business analysis practitioner tries to determine the business need (the "why") before determining the outcome (the "what") and how the company will achieve it (the "how"). Starting with answers to the "why" is what should be strived for if organizations are to achieve their goals and be successful.

The Golden Circle model (see Figure 2-1) helps an organization identify its "why" (business need or value proposition) and distinguish between it and the solution, which prevents rushing to a solution without a deep understanding of the "why."

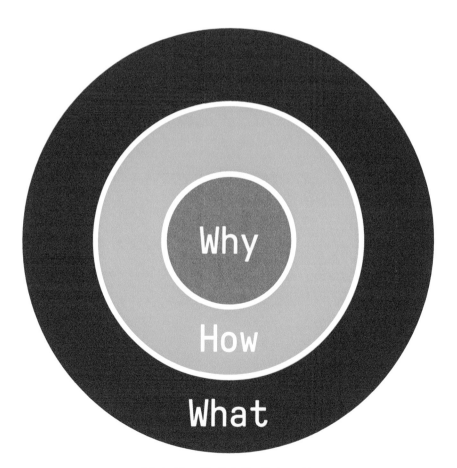

Adapted from Sinek's Golden Circle model.

Figure 2-1. Golden Circle Model

How to Understand the Situation

To achieve a deep understanding of the full context of the situation, an organization should elicit information relevant to the situation, including:

- Signs of problems and opportunities;
- Related stakeholders;
- Severity or magnitude of the situation;
- Situation statement;
- Root causes; and
- Business goals and objectives.

For each aspect of the situation (see Figure 2-2), different tools and techniques can be used to elicit the required information.

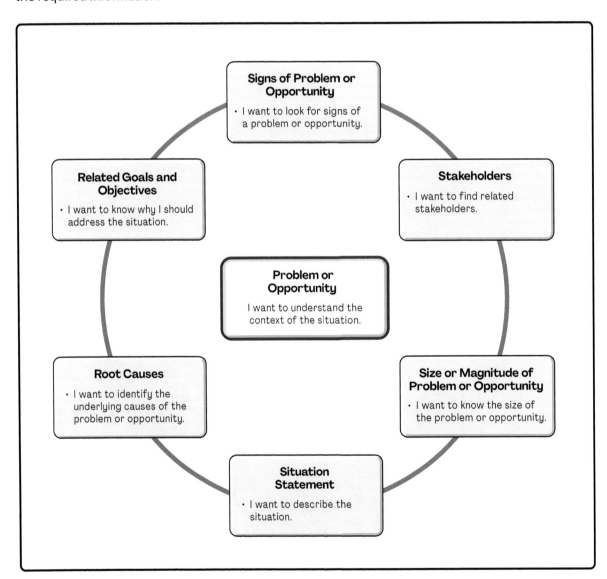

Figure 2-2. Eliciting Information to Understand the Situation

Signs of Problems and Opportunities

The business analysis practitioner focuses on learning enough about the problem or opportunity to adequately understand the situation.

Not every problem or opportunity needs consideration or attention. Practitioners should elicit more information about the context of the situation to understand whether the situation is worthy of further action.

Various types of elicitation techniques—such as interviewing, document analysis, observation, empathy maps, competitive analysis and market analysis, benchmarking, and data analysis—may be conducted to draw out sufficient information to fully identify the problem or opportunity.

In addition, data from evaluating the solution performance when reviewing implemented or partially implemented solutions may reveal whether the business value expected by the organization is being delivered. A significant variance between expected and actual value may indicate a potential problem or opportunity that needs to be addressed.

Related Stakeholders

Business analysis stakeholders are individuals, groups, or organizations that may impact, are impacted by, or have yet to be impacted by a problem or opportunity under assessment.

To get a robust understanding of the situation, it is important to find stakeholders related to the problem or opportunity as they will provide various insights into the situation.

The following are some techniques to help identify the appropriate stakeholders:

- Customer journey map;

- Brainstorming;

- Interviews;

- Document analysis; and

- Observation.

Questions that help identify stakeholders include:

- Who is negatively impacted by the problem or opportunity?

- Who benefits from the problem or opportunity?

- Who is involved in the situation?

- Who is affected by the situation?

- Who can influence the situation?

- Who is the final authority of the situation?

Severity or Magnitude of the Situation

Once a broad understanding of the situation is obtained, it is necessary to gather relevant data and information—for example, market size, trends, growth rates, customers, products, and distribution channels—to understand the magnitude of a problem or opportunity and determine an appropriate solution.

Lack of evaluation may result in proposing solutions that are either too small or too large for the situation at hand. Data analysis or benchmarking can be used for evaluating the situation and finding the magnitude of the problem or opportunity.

For example, the turnover rate of human resources is a problem for a company, but the severity of this problem depends on the type of human resources. If a company loses knowledge workers, even a 5% turnover rate is too much; however, that company might not see a problem with a 5% turnover rate for other types of workers.

Comparing these metrics to the average for the industry, and collecting and analyzing the relevant data, can provide valuable insight into the extent of the situation.

Situation Statement

A situation statement is an objective statement about a problem or opportunity that includes the statement itself, the situation facing the organization, and the resulting impact. A business analysis practitioner may use a variety of formats, such as a value proposition, for drafting a situation statement. What is important is not so much the format, but rather that the stakeholders and the team discuss and agree on the situation before exploring solutions. Drafting a situation statement provides a solid understanding of the problem or opportunity the organization wants to address.

Once the situation statement is drafted, the business analysis practitioner obtains agreement from relevant stakeholders previously identified. It may be necessary to revise or reword the situation statement until the stakeholders agree. This is an important step because the statement guides further work to assess the business need. If such approval is skipped, it is difficult to determine if the essence of the current situation has been captured. Failure to obtain the views and approval of all stakeholders may result in a solution that only addresses part of the business need or fails to satisfy it at all.

A common way to capture a situation statement is in three parts:

- **Part one: The problem/opportunity.** The problem/opportunity is the primary concern to be addressed.

- **Part two: The direct effect.** The direct effect serves as a link between the problem and the business impact. It is normally the most noticeable aspect of the situation—what can be seen or perceived.

- **Part three: The business impact.** The business impact is what a problem or opportunity costs the organization (if it is a problem that needs fixing) or might return to the organization (if it is an opportunity). It may be tangible or intangible. The situation statement does not need to detail the business impact; it just identifies it clearly for the stakeholders. An example is shown in Figure 2-3.

Guidelines for developing a situation statement include the following:

- Get the group together.

- Make sure all stakeholders are on the same page with what is being discussed.

- Don't worry if the situation statement is not perfect—the purpose is to achieve consensus regarding the problem.

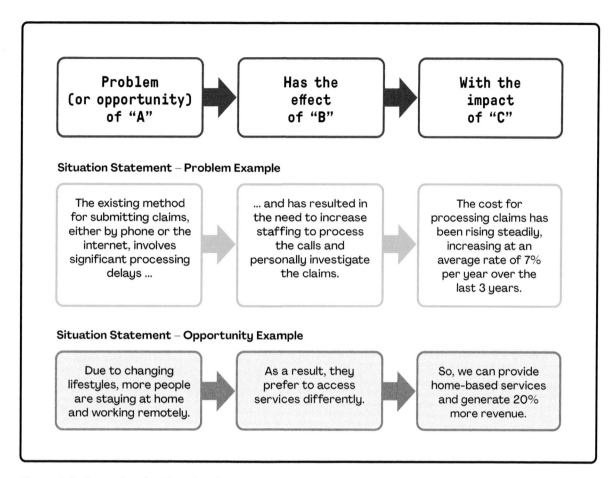

Figure 2-3. Example of a Situation Statement

- Ask the group to focus on the business problem and not to offer solutions.

- End the process when consensus is reached—the stakeholders will feel like their perspectives were validated.

Root Cause

Once a situation is discovered, documented, and agreed upon, it needs to be analyzed before being acted upon. After agreeing on the problem to be solved, the business analysis practitioner breaks it down into its root causes or opportunity contributors in order to adequately recommend a viable and appropriate solution. It also helps to validate the situation statement to ensure the right problem or opportunity has been found. Depending on what is found in the root cause analysis, stakeholders can revisit the situation statement.

There are various techniques to analyze the causes of a problem in depth and find the root cause, including but not limited to:

- Fishbone (Ishikawa) diagrams;

- Five whys;

- Interrelationship diagrams;

- Process analysis, including SIPOC (suppliers, inputs, process, outputs, and customers) and value stream maps; and

- Pareto charts.

Goals and Objectives

Existing organizational goals and objectives should be reviewed as part of the problem/opportunity identification to validate findings. Organizational goals and objectives are often revealed in internal corporate strategy documents and business plans. These information sources may be reviewed to acquire an understanding of the industry and its markets, the competition, products currently available, potential new products, and other factors used in developing organizational strategies. If corporate strategy documents and plans are not available for review, it may be necessary to interview stakeholders to determine this information.

When goals and objectives are not specified or are unclear, the business analysis practitioner documents them to establish the basis for subsequent work that relies on them. Objectives are often said to be "SMART" as summarized in Figure 2-4. Note there are subtle variations for what SMART means; this example is one of the more common definitions used.

Figure 2-5 shows an example of the hierarchical relationship between goals, objectives, and business cases, and various tactical plans to support them. The approved business cases are used as inputs to programs and projects; not all projects, however, have a formal business case associated with them.

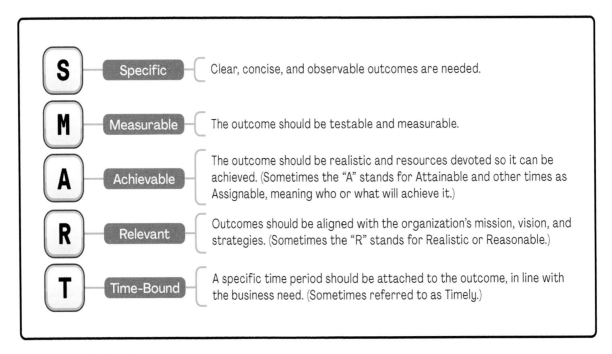

Figure 2-4. SMART Objectives

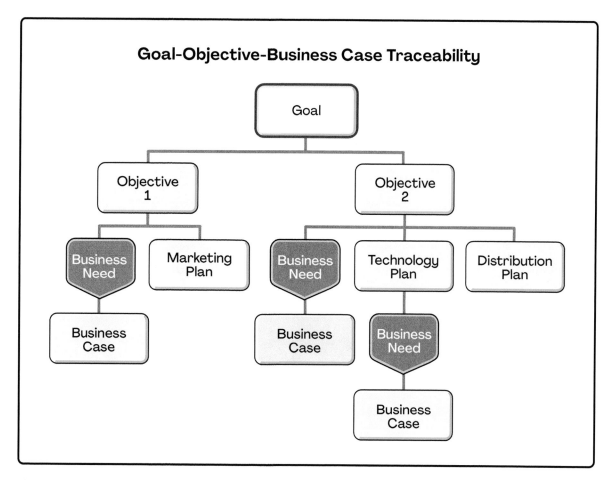

Figure 2-5. Goal-Objective-Business Case Traceability

Case Study: Understand the Situation

The Sustainable Construction Company (SCC) is a construction company that specializes in building environmentally friendly and sustainable homes. SCC expanded its market to a new region 2 years ago to increase sales and grow its presence in other climates. The company set a goal to build and sell 125 homes in this region within 1 year. About 6 months have passed, and only 25 homes have been sold. By this time, they expected 50 homes to be sold.

Since this trend means that objectives will not be met by the end of the year, leadership asked the business analysis team to investigate the situation and recommend an appropriate solution.

George and Rani are lead business analysis practitioners at SCC. They collaborate to gain a better understanding of the situation. They conduct several online and in-person interviews and analyze business analysis artifacts from the initial launch and organizational strategic documents to identify business goals and objectives.

(Continued)

Based on SCC strategic documents, George and Rani identify the following:

- **Vision:** To be recognized for bringing leading-edge, sustainable, and affordable housing technology to all people around the world.

- **Mission:** To build modern, affordable, and sustainable homes for people and families around the world.

- **Slogan:** "Build it for living, keep it for life."

- **Objectives:**

  o Sell 125 houses before the end of the year.

  o Generate revenue of US$60 million with a 40% profit margin.

Through their interviews and document analysis, George and Rani also identify the stakeholders and create an initial stakeholder register as shown in Table 2-1.

Table 2-1. Stakeholder Register

Stakeholder	Attitude	Level of Impact	Level of Influence	Communication Preferences	Location
Government agencies	Neutral	Low	High	Written formal	Government offices
SCC business owners	Positive	High	High	Written formal	Central office
Current homeowners	Negative	High	Low	Face to face	Houses in current region
Potential homebuyers	Neutral	Medium	Medium	Face to face	Cities near this region
Sales and marketing team	Neutral	Low	High	Email	Local office and central office
Community members	Negative	Low	Low	Social media and advertising	Cities near this region

Through the elicited information, they identify the initial elements of the situation to gain an understanding of the problem to share with stakeholders.

Situation Statement Elements:

- *Problem*—Residents are not interested in the houses.

- *Effect*—The houses are not selling as expected.

- *Impact*—The objective of selling 125 houses by the end of the year is in jeopardy.

As they continue to investigate, George and Rani learn that the SCC homes have been poorly received in the new climate zone where the company has tried to expand. Unlike residents in the moderate climate regions where the homes have been introduced, residents in this new climate zone have shown little interest in the SCC product, as evidenced by poorly attended open houses, few brochures and information packets being taken where available, and very little traffic at the model home.

The effect of this has been waste in the form of unused building materials, frustrated staff who developed the strategic initiative to move into this climate zone, and missed sales and failed marketing efforts.

The impact on SCC has been loss of momentum on the business objective to expand SCC homes into all global climate zones and missed sales goals of 125 houses by the end of the year.

They collaborate with stakeholders to develop the situation statement.

Situation Statement:

Residents in the new region in which SCC has built homes are not interested in the homes. This has resulted in failed sales and marketing efforts and put the SCC objective of selling 125 houses in this region by the end of the year in jeopardy.

George conducts a workshop with cross-functional stakeholders from different departments, who contribute to understanding the situation and analyze the causes of the problem. Rani participates as the scribe. During the workshop, George uses a *fishbone diagram* with *five whys* analysis to investigate the potential causes of the business problem. At the end of the workshop, he presents the results as shown in Figure 2-6.

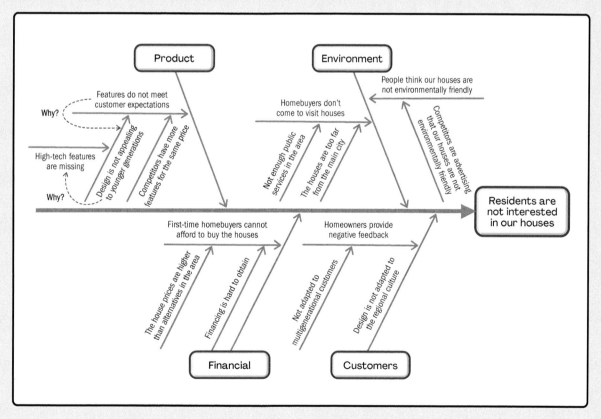

Figure 2-6. Fishbone Diagram Using Five Whys to Investigate Root Cause(s) of a Business Problem

Find the Gaps

The business analysis mindset turns the business analysis practitioner's attention to understanding the organization's current capabilities and the expectations for the future state by being open to information, listening to stakeholders, and asking probing questions. The practitioner's relentless curiosity ensures that the full context of the change is recognized.

Overview

Once the root causes of the situation have been explored, consensus about the situation has been achieved, and the goals agreed upon, the business analysis practitioner facilitates understanding of the existing state and elicits ideas about the desired state of the organization. This helps to identify what elements of the current state should remain unchanged and what changes are needed to achieve the future state. This is referred to as "Find the Gaps" (see Figure 2-7).

The business analysis practitioner proceeds to find the gaps in capabilities and the performance indicators, such as key performance indicators (KPIs) or objectives and key results (OKRs). These gaps refer to the missing capabilities and performance that the organization needs to acquire to address the business need in the future state. Analyzing the gap between the current capabilities and desired capabilities can reveal the missing capabilities in various areas such as people, processes, technology, and products. The difference between the desired and actual performance indicators is another important gap. This analysis can reveal how close the organization is to the desired performance indicators and can help define and set new objectives and targets.

Once the gaps have been identified, the business analysis practitioner performs further elicitation and analysis. This defines the changes needed to meet the business need and fulfill the missing capabilities to determine which existing capabilities should be retained and/or which new capabilities should be added.

The result of this practice is the list of net changes that the organization needs to make to achieve the desired future state. The capabilities and features listed do not provide a solution. Further analysis is required to determine how these capabilities and features will be delivered.

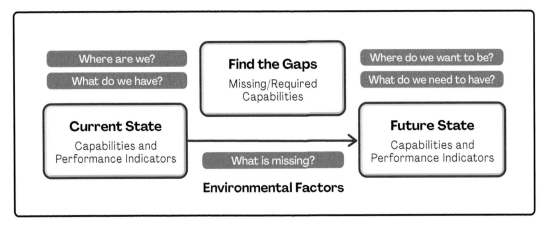

Figure 2-7. Find the Gaps Diagram

Value of Finding the Gaps

The primary benefit of performing Find the Gaps is to identify a set of capabilities that the business needs in order to move from the current state to the desired future state to meet business needs and generate business value. This approach provides information to guide decision makers, which can lead to better decisions and identification of the best places to deploy resources, focus energy, and prioritize recommendations.

Before proposing solution options, the business analysis practitioner identifies the current capabilities of the organization to include those that may be leveraged to meet the business need or new capabilities that need to be added.

For example, a company may have the resources or capabilities necessary to solve a problem through process improvement or staff restructuring. Or it may have those capabilities, or some of them but at a lower maturity level, and need to fill those gaps by leveling up through training or process improvement. In these cases, the solutions are usually simple to define, though not always easy to accomplish.

In some situations, it may be sufficient to recommend process changes without adding new capabilities or other resources. In more complicated situations, new capabilities and skills may be required, such as software, machinery, skilled employees, physical locations, or real estate. The business analysis practitioner should recommend appropriate capabilities based on discoveries made during root cause analysis or concepts and success factors that were identified during analysis of an opportunity.

How to Find the Gaps

The following steps broadly outline what may be done to find the gaps:

- Determine the area to be analyzed based on the situation statement and root causes identified.

- Identify internal and external factors directly related to the situation being analyzed. Analysis methods such as PESTLE (political, economic, social, technological, legal, environmental), CATWOE (customer, actor, transformation, worldview, owner, environment), and others may be used for this purpose.

- Analyze the current state (capabilities and performance indicators).

  o Historical data are used to establish performance standards against which the current and future performance will be evaluated.

  o Historical data obtained from the current capability analysis are used to understand trends and determine which metrics are helpful guidelines to determine if a capability is performing as it should be in its current state.

  o Business capability analysis is a technique used to analyze performance in terms of processes, people capabilities, and other resources used by an organization to perform its mission.

- Determine the desired future state (capabilities and performance indicators).

  o Ideation, categorization, and analysis comprise the appropriate set of tools to determine the most effective capabilities needed.

  o A capability table is used to categorize current and desired capabilities based on root causes.

- Compare the current state to the desired state, describe the gap, and quantify the difference.

  o *Gap analysis.* Determine whether business requirements or objectives are being met and, if not, what steps should be taken to meet them.

Case Study: Find the Gaps

George and Rani get stakeholder agreement on the situation statement and the root cause, and the next step is to find the gaps between the current and desired state.

To help identify the current capability related to the root cause of the problem, they use a *capability table* and assess the current organizational capability in different aspects such as people, process, and technology (see Table 2-2).

Then they conduct a session to identify ideas around the required capabilities for the future state. To avoid individuals influencing one another, Rani facilitates a *brainwriting* session to generate ideas. George participates as a scribe. After collecting ideas from the session, Rani uses an *affinity diagram* to categorize the ideas based on their relationship to the root causes. George adds the final results in the last column of the completed capability table.

Table 2-2. Completed Capability Table

High-Level Cause	Root Cause	Current Capabilities/ Features	Required Capabilities/Features
Homeowners' negative feedback	Not adapted to multigenerational families	One bedroom Interior space is flexible—easy to modify	New house design based on customer preferences Facilities for multigenerational families More than two bedrooms
	Design is not adapted to customer culture	Good-size countertops Large windows	Design several types of houses based on customer needs Explore better materials Offer a redesign plan to current customers at lower prices Interior space is flexible—easy to modify
Homebuyers do not come to tour houses	There are not enough public services	Low-quality water Cellular access to internet only Fire station Road that connects community to the city Good connection with local government Quiet, safe community	High-quality water High-speed internet infrastructure Grocery stores More stable electricity Better and more frequent public transportation
	The houses are too far from the main city	Road that connects to the city Good connection with local government Quiet, safe community	Better road to handle community growth Connection with public transportation Easy access to main city (e.g., a "fast lane") New schools New education system Modern health facility

Table 2-2. Completed Capability Table (continued)

First-time homebuyers cannot afford to buy the houses	Financing is hard to obtain	International bank is one of our shareholders	Support from local banks to provide mortgages for SCC houses Financial facilitation for essential jobs
Features do not meet customers' expectations	High-tech features are missing	Partnership with an IoT (Internet of Things) company	New high-tech features Controlling appliances by voice Monitoring temperature with mobile app More modern houses
People don't think our houses are environmentally friendly	Competitor advertising implies that our houses are not environmentally friendly	House looks "average" rather than "expensive" Inexperienced sales forces	New marketing strategy to "sell our features" Experienced sales agents Marketing focus on eco-friendly product
		Small area with some plants	Larger green areas Special plants

Define the Solution

The business analysis mindset encourages the incorporation of ideas from different perspectives, relying on continuous communication with stakeholders to select the best options for the solution, and creating commitment to meeting the objectives and implementing the solution. The business analysis practitioner looks at each option holistically and systemically to identify both benefits and disbenefits of each option.

Overview

Once the gaps between the current and needed capabilities are identified, the next step is to define the solution. Business analysis practitioners synthesize the information obtained during the business value assessment to support the selection of the best portfolio components, programs, or projects by developing a decision package that includes various artifacts related to the solution definition and obtaining buy-in and approval from key stakeholders. The artifacts may include a business case, product roadmap, high-level solution/product scope, or benefits realization plan.

Value of Defining the Solution

Defining the solution is of great value to the business because it helps ensure the business does not implement the wrong solution. Stakeholders may propose solutions without fully understanding the context around the situation. Presenting the results of the business value assessment to key decision makers, along with the rationale explaining why the viable options are being chosen, can reduce the likelihood that an unfit solution will be chosen.

Key benefits of this practice include:

- Helping organizations to analyze portfolio components, programs, and projects in a consistent manner, enabling the decision makers to determine whether the solutions are worth the required investment;

- Providing alternatives to show that these alternatives were considered, and to anticipate objections from those who favor them (another reason for including alternatives is the preferred approach may not be acceptable);

- Validating the feasibility of proposed solutions and promoting the best course of action for executives and decision makers to meet the business goals and objectives;

- Developing the business case, which will pass valuable input to the charter during project or program initiation, providing the team and other stakeholders with a concise and comprehensive view of the business need and the approved solution to that need;

- Developing a roadmap to create and manage shared expectations among stakeholders for the deliverables and the potential order in which they will be delivered; and

- Developing a product/solution roadmap that allows stakeholder expectations to be managed in better ways. This enables business analysis practitioners to delay or defer decisions on stakeholders' needs to a later point in the life cycle instead of rejecting their needs, which helps to reduce stakeholder resistance.

How to Define the Solution

The following steps may be used when defining a solution (see Figure 2-8):

1. Determine the options and make the necessary recommendations by applying various analytical techniques to explore possible solutions to achieve the business objectives and determine which is the best possible option for the organization to pursue. To gain all stakeholders' agreement and approval on the solution, make recommendations to fill those gaps. Note that the needed features and functions are only one part of the recommendation that will include the total sum

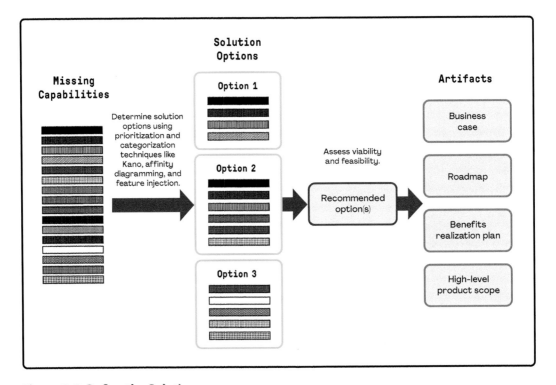

Figure 2-8. Define the Solution

of processes, systems, tools, people, and whatever else may be needed to deliver those features and functions and meet the business need.

2. For each potential option, perform an analysis to identify assumptions, constraints, risks, dependencies, intended benefits, and disbenefits related to those options.

3. Evaluate the feasibility and viability of each potential option to identify those options that may be discarded due to their infeasibility. The assessment should compare the potential solution options in terms of how viable each appears to be with respect to key variables or "feasibility factors."

4. Assemble the business case by collecting all of the information obtained in the business value assessment. Then package the information required by key decision makers to evaluate portfolio components, programs, or projects and decide whether they are worth pursuing. Develop a complete business case only for the most viable options to save valuable time.

5. Engage the team to determine the solution approach for each option. The solution approach is a high-level definition of the considerations and steps required to deliver the solution, and thus, transition the business from the current state to the future state. Through the development of a roadmap, the business analysis practitioner also provides a high-level approach to the deployment of the new capabilities, alternative approaches, feasibility of each alternative, and a preferred order of alternatives.

Recommended Options

After examining potential options for addressing a business need, the business analysis practitioner needs to recommend the most viable option (see Figure 2-9). If only one option is judged to be feasible after the analysis is completed, that option, in most cases, will be recommended. When there are no viable options to address the business need, one option is to recommend that nothing be done. When faced with two or more feasible options, the remaining choices can be arranged in

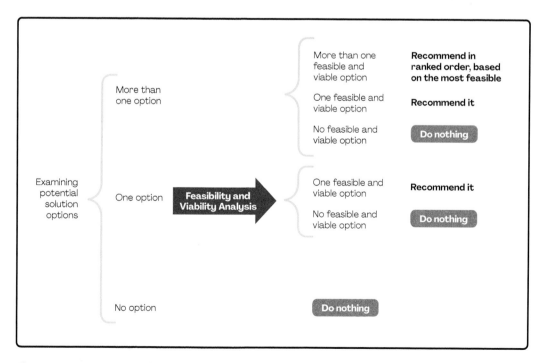

Figure 2-9. Recommending the Most Viable Option

ranked order, based on how well each one meets the business need. A technique such as multicriteria decision analysis (also known as weighted ranking) is a good choice to perform this analysis.

Product Roadmap. A complete recommendation includes a high-level proposal stating how the needed capabilities will be acquired. This approach is not a detailed project management plan and does not include the level of detail of a project charter. Instead, it is a suggested path for adding the capabilities. Product roadmaps provide important information about a product, offering insight about the product vision and how the product will support organizational strategy, business goals, and objectives over time.

The roadmap may have various formats. It could be a time line for adding high-level features to a solution, or a roadmap showing how to incorporate different potential solution options by keeping options open and deciding over time as information evolves using the real options technique.

The business analysis practitioner solicits preliminary feedback from the business and technical experts when the recommendation is going to include new or modified high-tech solutions.

Business Case. The business case presents information to establish whether the organization should address a problem or opportunity. It provides a documented feasibility study; establishes the validity of the benefits to be delivered by a project, program, or portfolio; and answers the question: "Why are we investing in this initiative?" The business case explores the nature of the problem or opportunity, presents its root causes or contributors to success, and looks at many facets contributing to a complete recommendation.

More than a simple input, a business case is a living document that is constantly referred to throughout a program or project. It may be necessary to review and update a business case based on what is discovered as a program or project progresses over time.

A minimum set of components in any business case should include the following:

- **Problem/opportunity.** Specification of what is prompting the need for action. Use a situation statement or similar way to document the business problem or opportunity to be addressed through a program or project. Include relevant data to assess the situation and identify which stakeholders or stakeholder groups are affected.

- **Analysis of the situation.** A list of organizational goals and objectives to assess how a potential solution supports and contributes to them. Include root cause(s) of the problem or main contributors of an opportunity. Support the analysis through relevant data to confirm the rationale. Include needed capabilities versus existing capabilities. The gaps between them will form the program or project objectives.

- **Recommendation.** The feasibility of each potential option. Specify any constraints, assumptions, risks, and dependencies for each option. Rank the alternatives and list the recommended one; include why it is recommended and why the others are not. Summarize the cost-benefit analysis for the recommended option. Include the implementation approach, including milestones, dependencies, roles, responsibilities, and change management considerations.

- **Evaluation.** A plan for measuring benefits realization. This plan typically includes metrics, including financial (such as ROI, sales, or others) and nonfinancial (such as Net Promoter Score® [NPS], turnover rate, and others) to evaluate how the solution contributes to organizational goals and objectives. Consider the time and cost of any additional work that may need to be done to capture and report those metrics.

The business analysis practitioner provides metrics for both benefits and disbenefits of the solution, describes how and when the benefits and disbenefits of the solution will be realized, and what mechanisms should be in place to measure them. Disbenefits should follow similar activities and processes as benefits management. They should be identified, categorized, quantified, and measured in the same manner as benefits.

Case Study: Define the Solution

Now, George and Rani collaborate with stakeholders to conduct a *gap analysis*. By working with stakeholders and comparing current capabilities to the required capabilities, they identify several gaps and, through discussion with stakeholders, identify solution components to fill those gaps and generate the missing capabilities. Using an *affinity diagram*, they classify the required capabilities into different categories based on similarity of development or context, as well as the root cause that each capability addresses. The result is seven solution options, as shown in Figure 2-10.

George and Rani conduct a *feasibility analysis* (see Table 2-3) for each solution option by identifying constraints, assumptions, and risks related to those options. They then evaluate each option in terms of operational, technological, financial, and time feasibility. During a workshop that includes

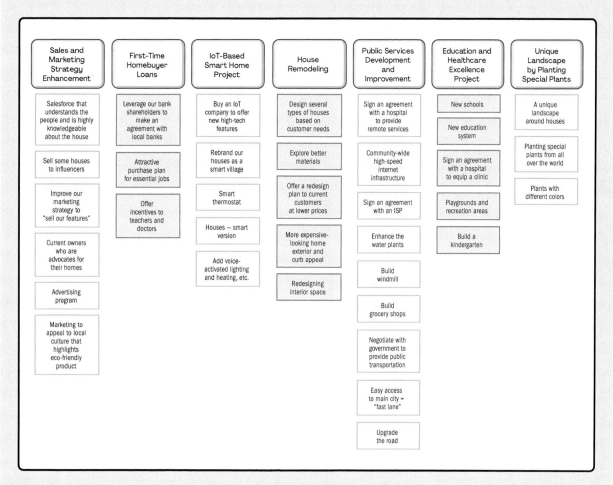

Figure 2-10. Affinity Diagram for Solution Options

(Continued)

Table 2-3. Feasibility Analysis Using Multicriteria Decision Analysis

Solution ID	Solution Name	Constraint	Assumption	Risk	Operational Feasibility	Technology Feasibility	Financial Feasibility	Time Feasibility	Score
					Weight of Feasibility Category				
					20%	20%	35%	25% Solution	
					Score (1–10) 1 = Low feasibility 10 = High feasibility If feasibility score is <5 in any category, option is not considered.				Weighted Score
Option A	House remodeling	The structure or supportive walls cannot be changed. The redesign will affect just the new houses that are going to be built.	The homeowner will pay part (%) of the renovation cost.	People may not buy the 24 houses that did not sell because of the new house design.	8	10	10	10	9.6
Option B	IoT-based smart home project	There are limited internet service providers (ISP) in this area.	Everyone uses a smartphone. The solution can use cellular service and any ISP.	The frequent power outages could affect IoT-based equipment (due to unstable climate).	8	7	9	10	8.6
Option C	Sales and marketing strategy enhancement	It has to be done after IoT-based project and redesign project (time constraints). SCC has budget limitations.	It is assumed that the other two projects are done before advertising starts.	Our competitors may respond with a more aggressive strategy or may change their strategy, based on SCC's current development.	6	10	10	6	8.2
Option D	First-time homebuyer loans	Not all customers are first-time homebuyers. There is not enough information about first-time homebuyers.	It is assumed that ABC Bank, which is an SCC shareholder, can make the deal with local banks.	There may not be enough first-time homebuyers.	6	10	8	8	8
Option E	Development of a unique landscape by planting special plants from around the world	SCC is going to use big plants; there are some limited ways to move them to this area.	SCC assumes that the nice landscape and special plants will attract people.	The plants may not last for a year because of the climate.	4	7	6	10	6.8
Option F	Public services development and improvement	There is a lack of specialists in this area to identify requirements for public services development.	SCC assumes that the government will cover a substantial part of the budget.	SCC may not get the labor for the developed public services.	7	7	5	7	6.3
Option G	Education and healthcare excellence project	SCC cannot lower the home prices more than 10%.	The assumption is that financial incentives will be sufficient to attract doctors and teachers.	The sales and marketing strategy may not attract doctors and teachers.	7	7	5	6	6.05

SCC owners, they assign a relative weight to each feasibility criterion and score each solution option accordingly.

Based on the feasibility analysis, the top two solution options with the highest score are identified as follows:

• Existing house remodeling project

• Internet of Things (IoT)-based smart home project

To illustrate the nonfinancial value and rationale for these projects, George and Rani conducted a *force field analysis* on the top options. Figure 2-11 is the result for the IoT-based smart home project.

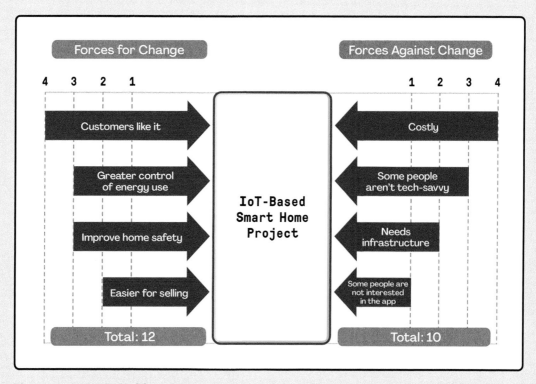

Figure 2-11. Force Field Analysis on Top Solution Options

Option E is rejected because it scores lower than 5 on operational feasibility. Options F and G are not financially feasible now, but could be if financing is obtained or more than 100 houses are sold before the end of the year. Using the *real options* technique, George and Rani identify two deadlines for decision-making regarding those options (see Figure 2-12):

• If a bonding bill passes and the government finances 70% of the initiative budget, or

• SCC sells more than 100 houses.

In this case, it will be feasible to move forward with the "public services development and improvement" initiative.

(Continued)

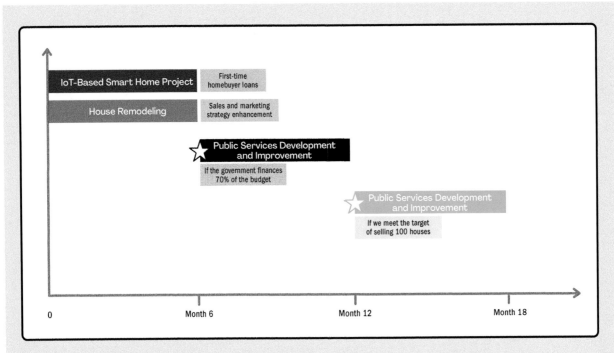

Figure 2-12. Product Roadmap

While working with senior leadership, including the sponsor and the nominated project managers on the business case, George and Rani reveal business objectives that were not previously defined.

Business objectives (BO):

- **BO1.** Generate a revenue of US$60 million with a 40% profit margin.

- **BO2.** Sell 125 houses before the end of Q2 of 20XX.

- **BO3.** Obtain a customer satisfaction NPS of ≥ 40.

George and Rani model the business and project objectives to confirm alignment as shown in Figure 2-13. (This may also be used later when elaborating and tracing in solution refinement.) They also update the benefits management plan as shown in Table 2-4.

They continue collaborating with leadership throughout these changes and assemble the business case and submit it to the SCC business owners for review and approval.

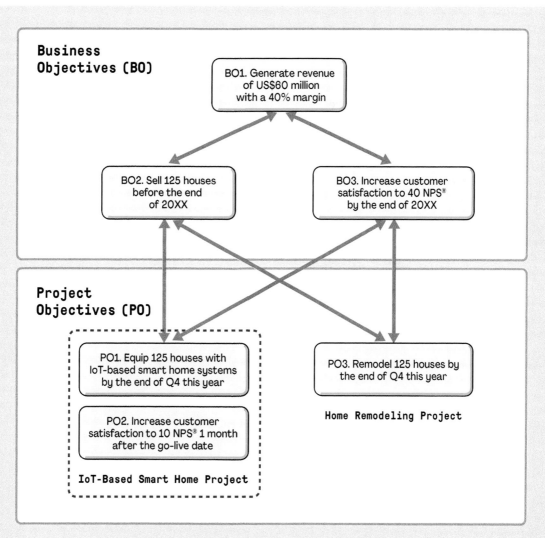

Figure 2-13. Business Objective and Project Objective Relationship

Table 2-4. Benefits Management Plan

Benefit	Metrics	Baseline	Target-Business Objective	Time Frame
Strong sales	Number of houses sold	25	125	By the end of Q2 of 20XX (check every 2 months)
Increased revenue	Generated revenue in US$	US$12 million with a 0% margin	US$60 million with a 40% margin	By the end of Q2 of 20XX (check every 2 months)
Customer satisfaction	NPS®	-30	40	Review 1 month and 6 months after adjustments are made to the new home (2 times)

3

Business Analysis Planning Domain

Introduction

How Business Analysis Planning is conducted depends heavily on the approach used for the initiative, whether predictive, adaptive, or hybrid. Appropriately scaled planning is foundational to the business analysis effort, whether that work is to be done all at once in the beginning of the initiative or iteratively throughout. The formality and degree of rigor used when planning will reflect the needs of the stakeholders, governance, and expected use of the planning outputs.

What to Expect in This Domain

Business Analysis Planning includes three practices that orient the business analysis practitioner and stakeholders to the business analysis work on the initiative. Whether done formally or informally, captured in a detailed plan, or understood as part of the regular cadence of adaptive work, every business analysis practitioner sets expectations with stakeholders regarding what to expect from the business analysis effort. The three key practices in this domain include:

- **Understand Business Analysis Governance** considers the internally and externally imposed regulations, rules, policies, and decision-making guidelines that will impact the business analysis work.

- **Determine Stakeholder Engagement Approach** identifies and assesses stakeholders, their relationships to the initiative, and what is helpful to know about them to engage them constructively in business analysis work.

- **Plan Business Analysis Work** explores the business analysis activities that will add value to the initiative and best address the business need, determines how much rigor and formality will be needed when executing those activities, and identifies the best way to set expectations for those activities.

Tailoring these practices will be most significantly impacted by the initiative approach, whether predictive, adaptive, or hybrid. Yet, even in a predictive environment, these practices will likely be iterative as governance, the stakeholder landscape, and the value proposition of the business analysis activities evolve.

Main Benefits of the Practices in This Domain

Planning business analysis work in collaboration with the right stakeholders, to the right level of detail, and at an appropriate level of formality given the organizational and initiative context, yields multiple benefits: Team members and other stakeholders have shared, clear expectations for the business analysis work to be done; activities are more likely to make good use of organizational time, which minimizes waste; and participants in business analysis activities are more engaged and supportive of the business analysis work.

Key Questions Answered in This Domain

- What are the governance frameworks to be considered when planning and executing business analysis activities?

- How does the business analysis practitioner identify and expect to engage with the stakeholders who will impact or be impacted by business analysis activities?

- What are the business analysis activities and how should they be scaled and tailored to add value within and beyond the boundaries of the initiative?

- How does the choice of an adaptive, predictive, or hybrid approach impact the business analysis planning and execution of business analysis activities?

Understand Business Analysis Governance

When understanding the approach to business analysis governance, a business analysis mindset helps the business analysis practitioner think comprehensively and holistically to lay the foundation for how business analysis work will be done.

Overview

Business analysis practitioners need to understand the business analysis guidelines, business rules, standards, and regulations that impact their initiatives. Depending on the industry, organization, complexity, and risk level of the solution, business analysis practitioners often need to collaborate with one or more roles within the governance category. Roles considered part of governance include legal, risk, release management, the change control board, DevOps (used to coordinate activities and improve collaboration between development and operational areas), project management office (PMO), value delivery office (VDO), business analysis center of excellence leader, or compliance auditors or officers.

These stakeholders provide important insights regarding regulations, auditing obligations, business rules, and required organizational processes the product team is obligated to support and comply with. Business analysis practitioners collaborate with these roles to ensure the product development process, including management of requirements and product information, is performed as required.

Governance impacts decision-making, including who makes decisions and when, and who approves key deliverables and when. The business analysis practitioner needs to clarify how decisions and approvals pertaining to requirements and product information, solution changes, and organizational transition (go/no-go) will be handled before those decisions and approvals are needed.

Many projects require little in the way of governance planning. Departmental, nonregulatory projects in small organizations may not have much governance that constrains their projects. Large, cross-functional, regulatory projects in regulated industries may have a lot of business analysis work that is required to be done as prescribed by one set of rules or another. Many aspects of governance, such as regulatory constraints, auditing obligations, and business rules, pertain to an initiative whether using a predictive or adaptive approach.

Value of Understanding Business Analysis Governance

Business analysis activities and decisions that are supportive of and consistent with governance frameworks help mitigate product and organizational risks related to noncompliance, including data security, information sharing, and legal risks. Conformance to required organizational processes may add efficiencies by utilizing language, processes, and practices that are shared and understood by others in the organization.

Identifying who is responsible for key decisions, including requirements approval, requirements priority, requirements change approval, and whether and when to move forward with implementation, mitigates conflict among stakeholders. Collaborating with stakeholders to define the who–what–when for decisions, before decisions are needed, helps expedite decision-making when the time comes and keeps the momentum focused on business analysis activities.

Understanding business analysis governance sets the business analysis practitioner up for success when planning how to engage stakeholders and conduct other business analysis activities. Time spent identifying and understanding relevant governance frameworks related to the definition, development, and implementation of a solution enables the business analysis practitioner to communicate them to stakeholders. This shared understanding means everyone can be a part of mitigating risk, minimizing waste, and contributing to the development of organizational business analysis good practices.

How to Understand Business Analysis Governance

Understanding business analysis governance frameworks is primarily investigative work to find out what mandatory policies, procedures, rules, or other aspects of governance need to be followed. It includes understanding the governance structures that may be relevant to business analysis work and important to stakeholders who have expectations for specific ways in which business analysis work is conducted. For this practice, business analysis practitioners connect with stakeholders throughout the organization as well as outside the organization (e.g., when external regulations will impact the initiative). Artifacts created or utilized may include policy documents from the organization's people or human resources (HR) function; project, program, or value management offices; external regulatory bodies; organizational business rules, catalogs, or repositories; or artifacts and records from previous projects. To confirm understanding of roles and responsibilities regarding business-analysis-related decisions, a responsibility assignment matrix may be created and shared.

Case Study: Understand Business Analysis Governance

The business case is approved by the senior leaders who collaborated during its development. The project manager who participated in the business case development then collaborates with the sponsor to develop project charters for the **house remodeling project** and the **IoT-based smart home project**.

George is identified as the lead business analysis practitioner for the house remodeling project, and he will be using a predictive approach. Rani is identified as the lead business analysis practitioner for the IoT-based smart home project, and she will be using an adaptive approach.

(Continued)

As the team is learning about the business case and starting to think about their business analysis work on the initiative, George and Rani take time to understand the governance their teams need to be aware of and the impact it will have on their business analysis efforts. SCC has a value delivery office (VDO), so George and Rani set up time to talk with the VDO about what the requirements are for business analysis work. George's last SCC project was under the guidance of the VDO, so he has a pretty good idea of how governance will impact the work on this project. He reviews his business analysis deliverables from the previous project, including the business analysis plan, as a starting point to identify the level of appropriate governance for his project. He identifies the following rules with which both George and Rani need to comply:

- Business analysis documents are required to be kept in an SCC online repository in the folder assigned to the project by the VDO.

- The business case is required to be reviewed quarterly, updated as necessary, and versioned quarterly.

- Business analysis deliverables, including the business analysis plan, requirements traceability matrix (if used), and responsibility assignment matrix, are to be read-only for everyone except the lead business analysis practitioner.

Since George's last project, the VDO has developed a *responsibility assignment matrix* that identifies the decision-making roles and responsibilities pertinent to business analysis work on all SCC projects using a predictive project approach (see Table 3-1).

It was agreed that digital signatures will be accepted for all approvals.

George confers with Rani to see what her thoughts are about governance for her IoT initiative. She confirms that since her team will be using an adaptive approach, decision-making will be handled as part of the process and determined by roles. Namely, the product owner will make all decisions in consultation with the development team.

Table 3-1. Governance Responsibility Assignment Matrix

Team Member	Key Decision or Type of Decision						
	Requirements Approval (Majority)	Requirements Approval Format	Requirements Priority (Majority)	Requirements Change Approvals	Requirements Change Approval Format	Go/No-Go Decision	Go/No-Go Decision Approval Format
Business analysis practitioner	C	–	C	C	–	C	–
Project manager	D	Email approval	C	C	–	D	Digital signature
Sponsor	S	Digital signature	S	S	Digital signature	D/S	Digital signature
Change control board	–	–	–	D/S	Digital signature	I	–
Construction lead	D	Email approval	D	C	–	D	Digital signature
Sales and marketing lead	D	Email approval	D	C	–	D	Digital signature

Key: D = Decision-making participant – vote on decision   S = Sign-off required (digital signature)
I = Informed about decision after it is made   C = Consulted before decision is made

Determine Stakeholder Engagement Approach

The business analysis mindset promotes the discovery of all stakeholders, including those who may not speak for themselves, and creatively utilizes different ways of gaining their involvement.

Overview

The term *stakeholder* implies that an individual defined as such is necessarily engaged. After all, they have a "stake" in what the organization is doing. As any project professional knows, assuming stakeholders are engaged can be risky. An initiative may be a high priority for those carrying it out, but those who are not directly involved have plenty of projects and other activities to steer their attention away from the initiative. Business analysis practitioners constantly compete for the attention of their stakeholders. The only way to get and keep their attention is with a well-formed and well-executed plan for determining the stakeholder engagement approach.

It is important to remember that planning this approach to engage stakeholders does not mean coming up with a fixed course of action. Business environments are evolving and may change quickly, particularly as they relate to stakeholders. People move or take different positions. Organizations change, transform, and reorganize. External environments are constantly in flux, pulling stakeholders in different directions—sometimes literally, such as when a global pandemic moved most office workers to remote work for an unspecified period of time.

The approach to stakeholder engagement needs to consider not only who and where the stakeholders are, but also the larger stakeholder context that impacts how their engagement will be achieved and sustained. For example:

- What are the stakeholders' expectations for business analysis activities?

- Do they know what good business analysis looks like?

- What are the stakeholders' preferred communication styles?

- How accessible are the stakeholders?

- What is the organizational culture like in terms of business analysis practices?

- What governance frameworks should be paid attention to, and are the stakeholders familiar with them?

It is impossible to think about every conceivable factor that will impact stakeholder engagement at one specific planning point in the initiative. Rather, an effective approach to engaging stakeholders should set the business analysis practitioner up for success by thinking through initial questions such as those mentioned previously and then maintaining awareness and curiosity about the stakeholder environment throughout the initiative. An effective business analysis practitioner should always be asking: "Is there anyone I am missing?" or "Am I losing interest from key stakeholders I need to be connected to right now?"

Value of Determining Stakeholder Engagement Approach

Engaging stakeholders may be the single most effective way for anyone to increase the likelihood of success—no matter how success is defined. Without engaged stakeholders, the most brilliant business analysis practices will yield little value; with engaged stakeholders, obstacles can be overcome, support through difficult times will be available, and shared goals will be realized. The relationship between disengaged stakeholders and lack of value is intricate, as is the relationship between engaged stakeholders and value-add activities and outcomes.

How to Determine Stakeholder Engagement Approach

Identifying, clarifying, prioritizing, and illustrating the evolving stakeholder landscape should be done throughout an initiative. A multitude of techniques are used for understanding and engaging stakeholders, the results of which may be captured in a stakeholder register or stakeholder engagement matrix.

Case Study: Determine Stakeholder Engagement Approach

To identify stakeholders related to the solutions, George and Rani create an *onion diagram* (see Figure 3-1) because it helps identify stakeholders at various levels—from the project team to those outside of the team and organization.

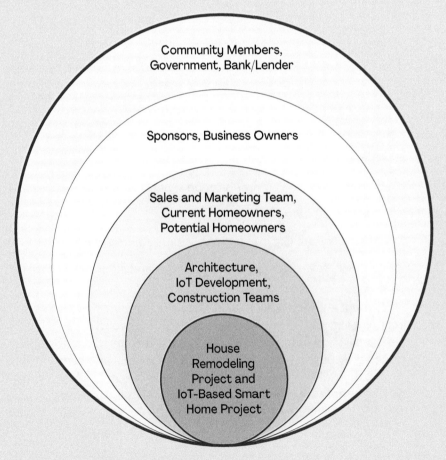

Figure 3-1. Stakeholder Onion Diagram

The layers of the case study onion diagram are:

- **Layer 1:** (optional core layer)—Beginning at the center, the initiative is identified.

  o   House remodeling project

  o   IoT-based smart home project

- **Layer 2:** Team that is executing the project or creating the product.

  o   SCC's architecture team

  o   SCC's IoT development team

  o   SCC's construction team

- **Layer 3:** Teams or individuals directly impacted by the change that will occur with the new initiative or product. An example is a team that will be using a new solution being introduced to the business.

  o   SCC's sales and marketing team

  o   Current homeowners

  o   Potential homeowners

- **Layer 4:** Teams or individuals who regularly interact with those in Layer 3. This layer could include sponsors, business owners, or others who interact with those who are impacted.

  o   Sponsors

  o   Business owners

- **Layer 5:** Any external stakeholders who can directly influence requirements or will be impacted by the changes brought about by the initiative or product. Examples are regulators, customers, or suppliers.

  o   Community members

  o   Government

  o   Bank or lender

Assess Stakeholder Engagement

Once the stakeholders are identified, George and Rani assess how these various stakeholders are involved in the current state and to what extent their involvement will need to be shaped to attain a successful future state in terms of the solutions. Given that their projects have very similar stakeholders, and to avoid redundancy, George and Rani collaborate with each other and their respective project managers to assess the engagement levels of their stakeholders. To support this assessment, they utilize a *stakeholder engagement assessment matrix*, shown in Table 3-2.

(Continued)

Table 3-2. Stakeholder Engagement Assessment Matrix

Stakeholder	Unaware	Resistant	Neutral	Supportive	Leading	Action	Owner
SCC business owners				Current Desired		Update and review the business case quarterly.	George (business analysis practitioner)
Sales and marketing team			Current		Desired	Offer bonus incentives based on increased sales. Plan more strategic advertising on houses.	Sales director
Architecture team		Current			Desired	SCC will fund the presentation of their final work at the Global Architecture Conference.	Architecture lead
IoT development team					Current Desired	Offer bonus incentives based on reported bugs and user satisfaction scores.	SCC business owners
Construction team			Current		Desired	Offer bonus incentives based on quality inspections.	Project manager
Potential homebuyers	Current				Desired	Offer IoT setup and free use for 1 year after home purchase.	Sales and marketing
Current homeowners		Current		Desired		Facilitate focus groups and offer incentives for participation. Subsidize house improvement for lower cost.	Sales and marketing
Community members		Current	Desired			Host educational open house with free refreshments and prizes.	Sales and marketing
Government agencies			Current		Desired	Ask newspaper for an article about the lack of public services.	Project manager
Banking lender			Current	Desired		SCC business owners sign agreements with bank lenders to provide financing.	SCC business owners

George and Rani consider the types of stakeholders and identify two key roles to focus on: existing homeowners and first-time homebuyers (see Figure 3-2 and Table 3-3). Because the number of homeowners and homebuyers are too many to consider individually, George and Rani work with the product owner on Rani's project, and the sponsor and key team members on George's project, to develop initial thoughts about customer profiles.

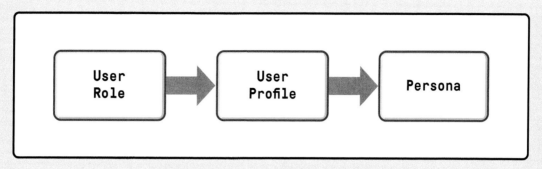

Figure 3-2. Developing Personas to Better Relate to Customers

Table 3-3. Customer Profiles (Existing and First-Time Homebuyers)

	Customer Profiles	
	Existing Homeowner	First-Time Homebuyer
Background: What are some typical characteristics of the person in this role?	This person is the head of household for the three or four generations living in the home, is the primary breadwinner, and is concerned with making the home safe and comfortable for everyone. This person wants to ensure that everyone is able to actively contribute to the family's day-to-day living.	The typical new homebuyer is a young, professional couple who uses their home as a base from which they travel for work and leisure.
Demographics: What are some demographics of the typical person in this role?	• Works full-time hours • 50–60 years of age • Expects to retire in the home someday and wants to enjoy retirement with their family in the house	• Works full-time hours • 35–40 years of age • Tech-savvy and quick to apply new technologies to their daily living • Engaged in climate change initiatives
Goals: What are the homeowner's goals related to the home?	They want the home to be a means of maintaining a traditional family structure as well as be flexible and modern enough to give all generations what they expect in today's modern home.	They are looking for their first home and want one that is easy to maintain and monitor when they are away. They have family and friends who come to visit and need to be able to accommodate them easily without disruption.
Pain points: What about the current state is problematic for the typical person in this role?	The kitchen does not allow for everyone to collaborate during meal preparation. The home is difficult for people with disabilities to navigate in some areas. The spaces are not flexible for closing off for use when working privately.	The current model is not appealing to this group as it is too traditional in style and does not offer technologies for the remote operation and monitoring of utilities and appliances.
Collaborators: Whose thoughts should be considered when making decisions about the home?	The homeowner's key collaborator is their spouse, who is also working and supports the household financially. The other family members also contribute to running the household and their needs are important to consider in order to maintain their interest in keeping the family under one roof.	This potential homebuyer consults with their partner and considers the needs of their family and friends when visiting.

(Continued)

George and Rani's teams use profiles to develop a couple of personas to make it easier for them to talk about and relate to the customers as they are working on the home remodeling and IoT-based smart home projects. They have some fun with the profiles and come up with the following:

- Henry, the head of household homeowner (see Figure 3-3)
- Sara, the tech-savvy, first-time homebuyer (see Figure 3-4)

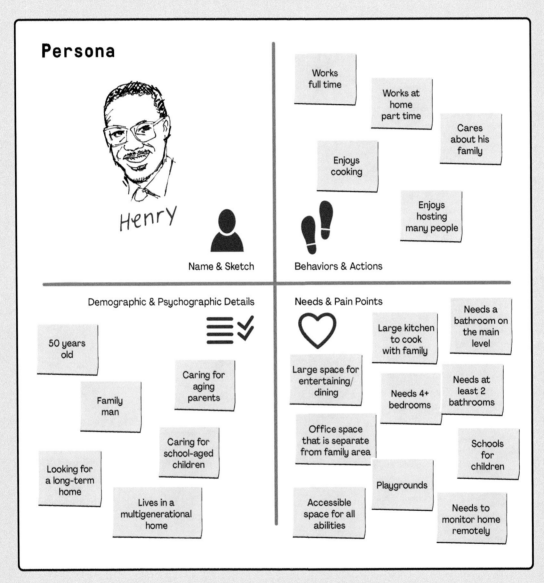

Figure 3-3. Persona for Henry, Head of Household Homeowner

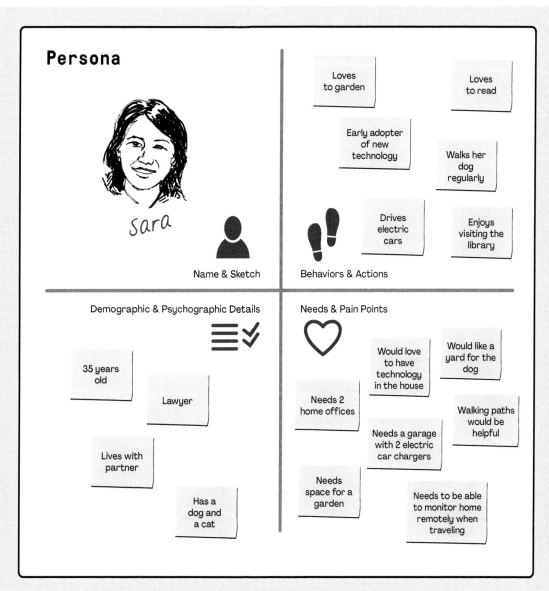

Figure 3-4. Persona for Sara, the Tech-Savvy, First-Time Homebuyer

Plan Business Analysis Work

A business analysis mindset provides a holistic and comprehensive perspective when planning business analysis work. It brings creativity to the exercise of scaling the work to be of high value, and only as much as is needed, to meet the needs of the stakeholders, the initiative, and the organization.

Overview

Business analysis activities occur within and outside of the context of projects or programs. When business analysis stakeholders are identified, it is possible that their engagement will be needed at various points in an initiative, as well as before or after. In addition, the variety of business analysis activities is considerable: eliciting, tracing, prioritizing, modeling, consensus building, scheduling, collaborating, evaluating, facilitating, etc.—the list is long. The degree of rigor as required by governance or other stakeholder needs can make the workload even heavier. So, it is the wise business analysis practitioner who asks the question: "What do I really need to do for this initiative?" Not all potential business analysis activities need to be done, and not all activities that need to be done require the same degree of formality or detail.

Plan Business Analysis Work means identifying what the business analysis practitioner or business analysis team anticipates doing and how much of it they need to do. This planning includes understanding the project approach being used and the organizational culture, so business analysis work is appropriately scaled and tailored to the context of the situation and organizational environment. Whether done formally or informally, an assessment of potential work sheds light on which activities will add value and which could be useful but would take more time or effort than they are worth. Planning also considers when the value-add business analysis work may be done and with whom.

The business analysis plan is focused on the scope of the business analysis effort. This includes a list of the activities to be conducted and the business analysis deliverables to be produced. A list of the roles required to successfully conduct the business analysis process is included in the business analysis plan. Key process decisions are also included, such as the approach for prioritizing, documenting, validating, communicating, approving, and changing requirements.

Whether documented formally or agreed upon informally by team members, the business analysis practitioner generates a clear and shared understanding of planning decisions, so stakeholders know what to expect when business analysis activities begin. Where team members disagree with one or more of the decisions being made, the business analysis practitioner facilitates negotiations and brings the team to a consensus or participates as a team member to help the team come to agreement. Once decisions are made, it is often helpful to document them so conflicts do not resurface later when the business analysis work is being performed. Some high-performing teams working in adaptive or less formal environments may already be working with a shared understanding of clearly understood activities and decisions as a part of their process, in which case business analysis planning decisions may be captured as part of a teaming or working agreement, or possibly not documented at all.

When written, the business analysis plan needs to be easily understood because it will be reviewed and may need to be approved by key stakeholders. When documenting the business analysis plan, it is a good practice to provide explanations for the planning choices made. For example, for projects using an adaptive life cycle, the depth and cadence of analysis activities will be planned much differently than for projects using a predictive approach. The prioritization process, types of techniques, and deliverables will vary. Explaining why planning choices were selected provides context for those who review the plan and provides the rationale for the decisions made.

Decisions made as a part of business analysis planning include the following, many of which are influenced by the approach used, either predictive, adaptive, or hybrid:

- Type of elicitation activities to be conducted;

- Requirements analysis models to be used;

- How requirements will be documented and communicated to stakeholders, including the use of any specialized tools;

- Business analysis deliverables to be produced;

- Roles and responsibilities for those participating in the requirements-related activities;

- How requirements will be prioritized, approved, and maintained;

- List of requirements that will be tracked and managed in the requirements documentation, such as business requirements document (BRD) or requirements traceability matrix (RTM);

- How requirements will be validated and verified;

- How the acceptance criteria will be determined for the requirements and solution validation;

- What aspect of the solution will be evaluated; and

- How, when, and who will evaluate the solution.

Value of Planning Business Analysis Work

Plan Business Analysis Work provides a roadmap for the activities to be performed. The roadmap is a valuable tool for the business analysis practitioner to set expectations with stakeholders regarding how and when they will collaborate to achieve the goal. Like any roadmap, there will be detours and obstacles, so the stakeholders can expect the roadmap to change. In fact, an initial plan may only address the early phase(s), iteration(s), or milestone(s) of a project. The plan is a starting point to create a shared understanding of the journey that involves all stakeholders.

Planning business analysis work sets expectations for stakeholders as well as the business analysis practitioner and team. It is tempting to consider performing all of the potential business analysis work that could be done, but that may or may not be practical. Planning requires the business analysis practitioner to take a realistic, pragmatic view of what makes sense, so they can be good stewards of the stakeholders' time and make reasonable commitments.

Finally, having some level of a plan is what enables flexibility. In the absence of a plan, people struggle to know what is happening next or what is expected of them. Not having a plan contributes to an atmosphere of uncertainty and confusion, where each individual tries to find a direction. When everyone is working from the same plan, even one that is high level, everyone is aware of what needs to be done, has a sense of which parts of the plan will or will not work, understands options for deviating from the plan, and knows which way leads to success. Solid, well-scaled plans contribute to environments with confident, flexible partners who are better able to collaborate.

How to Plan Business Analysis Work

Plan Business Analysis Work, like everything a business analysis practitioner does, should be done collaboratively to ensure the needs of the stakeholders, the initiative, and the organization will be met. In particular, collaborating with a project or program manager, project management office (PMO), or value delivery office (VDO), if available, enhances the effectiveness and efficiency of planning business analysis work.

Case Study: Plan Business Analysis Work

Before beginning elicitation and analysis, George and Rani consider their approach to the business analysis work to be done on their initiatives. They identify what will add value to their projects and how much rigor they need to apply given their stakeholders, risks to the business analysis work, and development approach. They include the business analysis team and other key stakeholders in their planning to promote ownership, gain buy-in for the work to be done, and set a collaborative tone for their projects.

Because George is using a more formal, predictive approach, he expects to have scheduled elicitation sessions, utilize a requirements traceability matrix, capture requirements in a business requirements document, and develop a schedule that is consistent in detail with how the project manager is developing their schedule.

Rani is using an adaptive approach and spends only as much time as she needs to get started and then plans regularly throughout the iterations as the project progresses.

They both confirm the approach to their work with the project manager and value delivery office (VDO) to ensure adherence to SCC governance and that they are appropriately scaling their work. They identify the key deliverables that will be needed, given their respective approaches (see Table 3-4).

Table 3-4. Deliverables for George and Rani

George	Rani
Business analysis plan	Product backlog
Business requirements document	User stories
Requirements traceability matrix	Definition of done (DoD)
Business rules catalog	Acceptance criteria
Models	Iteration length
Transition plan	Iteration plan
Readiness checklist	
Requirements change control approach	

The following key activities are identified:

- Elicitation (George)
  - o Focus groups
  - o Workshops
  - o Interviews
  - o Benchmarking
  - o Modeling
- Tracing
- Prioritizing
- Validating
- Verifying
- Obtaining approval for baseline
- Evaluating the solution
- Defining and sharing the requirements change control approach

Rani conducts planning informally with her team and in working sessions throughout the iterations. She does a lot of planning, but it is embedded in the regular cadence of her work, rather than at specific points in time.

Through consultation with Rani and the other team members, George comes up with a high-level plan for the work to be done on his project (see Table 3-5).

Table 3-5. High-Level Business Plan Template

Reference	Business Analysis Planning	Weeks							
		1	2	3	4	5	6	7	8
1	Create business analysis plan								
2	Elicit requirements								
2.1	Conduct focus groups, workshops, and interviews								
2.2	Research industry benchmarks and standards								
2.3	Research regulatory documentation								
3	Create models								
4	Gain consensus on new building materials								
5	Create business requirements document								
6	Prioritize requirements								
7	Maintain requirements traceability matrix								
8	Create business rules catalog								
9	Create transition plan								
10	Create readiness checklist								
11	Document requirements change control approach								
12	Hand off requirements to architecture team								

4

Solution Refinement Domain

Introduction

Solution Refinement consists of the iterative business analysis work that is performed to elaborate requirements and other solution information, so stakeholders are able to make decisions about the solution details and team members are able to develop it. This domain describes how the information is collaboratively elicited, decomposed, and organized using various models before being presented, to assess whether and how to move forward.

What to Expect in This Domain

This domain highlights key practices when refining the solution details, including requirements. The practices in Solution Refinement are performed iteratively throughout any endeavor that entails business analysis to ensure that the requirements are sufficiently elicited, analyzed, and presented to stakeholders in a fashion that fits their purpose. The three key practices in this domain include:

- **Elicit Solution Information** ensures that the information elicited is complete and represents the real needs of the stakeholders and not only their stated or perceived needs.

- **Analyze Solution Information** ensures that the information is well organized and prioritized to clarify scope, address assumptions, and eliminate gaps in stakeholders' understanding of the solution.

- **Package Solution Information** ensures high-quality solution information to enable stakeholders to make decisions with confidence about their understanding.

These practices occur continuously and iteratively throughout the business analysis effort. Elicitation can uncover anything, and anything can be analyzed. Therefore, these practices apply everywhere solution information is found and processed.

Main Benefits of the Practices in This Domain

The benefit of applying the practices of Solution Refinement is the confidence that the information elicited, and its contribution to the clarification of the scope and assumptions, is complete and sufficiently clear to stakeholders, resulting in increased trust in the decisions made.

Key Questions Answered in This Domain

- What should be considered when performing elicitation of the solution requirements?

- When does elicitation occur?

- What can be analyzed?

- What types of modeling will be most valuable?

- How will solution information best be presented to stakeholders?

Elicit Solution Information

Employing a business analysis mindset when eliciting solution information helps the business analysis practitioner discover and understand stakeholder needs and requirements before jumping to solutions. This mindset, combined with knowledge and experience, also enables the business analysis practitioner to lead and facilitate activities more effectively, resulting in better outcomes.

Overview

Elicitation is the iterative activity of drawing out information from stakeholders and other sources. In business analysis, it involves partnering with stakeholders to work together to discover the causes of the business problem or the reasons for addressing a current opportunity, as well as the information that will eventually be used to sufficiently refine requirements that enable solution development and implementation.

A substantial part of the business analysis practitioner's overall effort will be spent helping stakeholders define the business problem or opportunity and determine viable options for what could be done to address it. Requirements are not necessarily formed in the minds of stakeholders, and therefore, are not always available for "collecting" or "gathering." They have wants and needs but may not be able to express them clearly. They may know there is a problem but may need to collaborate to determine the root causes and how best to address them. Similarly, they may want to take advantage of an opportunity but do not know how to get started.

When conducting elicitation, business analysis practitioners use their mindset, skills, subject matter knowledge, and professional experience to empower stakeholders to clearly describe their ideas and carefully consider their needs and requirements. Effective business analysis practitioners also pay attention to the impact of elicitation within different business environments, industries, and cultures to design diverse activities that use models, methods, and artifacts that will generate the most engagement and achieve the best results.

Elicitation in every environment, whether predictive, adaptive, or hybrid, is an iterative activity impacting the entirety of the business analysis effort. In adaptive environments, business analysis practitioners can support, serve as a proxy, and even fill the role of a product owner, particularly regarding elicitation activities. The business analysis practitioner's understanding of the business problem, and alignment of the solution with the business strategy, solution requirements, and key stakeholders, puts them in a position to serve effectively in that capacity.

When working with the product owner in an adaptive environment, the business analysis practitioner shares their elicitation expertise when developing and refining the product backlog. Progressively elaborating the product backlog items to be sufficiently detailed for the team to develop is the responsibility of the product owner, and it is done well through the application of business analysis techniques with which the product owner may not be experienced. The business analysis practitioner, working with or filling the role of product owner, will likely have access to parts of the organization they would not otherwise, and can glean necessary information and resources to ensure that the solution meets stakeholder needs and adds value to the business.

Value of Eliciting Solution Information

Eliciting solution information is fundamental to identifying and clarifying everything from the business need to the high-level details of the solution, to development-ready functional requirements. Together with analysis, elicitation turns needs and expectations into something that can be analyzed, measured, tested, and ultimately delivered. Eliciting is done throughout the domains of business analysis. Examples include:

- **Business Value Assessment** is where elicitation is central to "Understand the Situation" to help define the problem and gather information from the organization's leadership to align the problem or opportunity to goals and objectives. "Find the Gaps" includes elicitation to define current and future states and determine how to bridge the gaps. "Define the Solution" necessitates elicitation to assess the feasibility and viability of solution options.

- **Business Analysis Planning** is when elicitation is done to discover who the stakeholders are and how best to meet their needs in the context of the project. "Understand Business Analysis Governance" requires eliciting to understand how decisions are made and define processes that will enable decision-making in the context of the initiative. "Determine Stakeholder Engagement Approach" requires eliciting stakeholders' communication needs and identifying how to engage them. Elicitation is central to "Plan Business Analysis Work" when identifying which business analysis activities will add value and determining how to tailor them.

- **Solution Transition and Evaluation** is where elicitation is required to determine what is needed to move the solution forward. "Enable Solution Transition" involves eliciting to define transition requirements. "Facilitate Go/No-Go Decision" involves eliciting to help stakeholders reach a consensus on moving forward with the solution. "Evaluate Solution Performance" involves eliciting to confirm understanding of the performance metrics to help stakeholders understand whether the solution is providing the value expected.

- **Business Analysis Stewardship** is where business analysis practitioners elicit to understand stakeholders' expectations for business analysis performance as part of "Promote Business Analysis Effectiveness." Elicitation is used in "Enhance Business Analysis Capability" to find out how people see themselves as practitioners. In "Lead Business Analysis with Integrity," elicitation is used to surface ethical concerns about activities, outputs, or outcomes to make them transparent to stakeholders.

How to Elicit Solution Information

There are three steps to elicitation with stakeholders:

1. Prepare to elicit.
2. Conduct elicitation.
3. Document elicitation output.

Prepare to Elicit

When preparing to elicit, business analysis practitioners, based on the approach, coordinate activities to understand which stakeholders will participate and how. Formally preparing for elicitation may be negligible or even unlikely in some environments or circumstances. For example, in adaptive environments, elicitation is a steady, ongoing activity. Even in predictive environments, savvy business analysis practitioners are always ready to elicit relevant information when the opportunity presents itself, whether they have formally prepared or not.

Prior to conducting elicitation, business analysis practitioners should prepare questions to ensure that time is well spent and the session objectives are achieved. It can be effective to share the questions prior to the session so the stakeholders have time to gather their thoughts and will not feel pressured.

It is important to note that not all questions are planned; much of the conversation during elicitation, while directed and investigative in nature, is spontaneous. It is the business analysis practitioner's job to guide it so the desired outcomes of the session can be met. Questions generally fall into four categories:

- **Open-ended questions:** Questions that allow respondents to answer in any way they desire.

- **Closed-ended questions**: Questions that call for a response from a limited list of answer choices. Types of closed-ended questions are forced choice, limited choice, and confirmation.

- **Contextual questions**: Questions that require an answer regarding the subject at hand— namely, the problem domain or the proposed solutions.

- **Context-free questions**: Questions that may be asked in any situation. Context-free questions are also used as lead-ins to obtain information to define the solution.

Conduct Elicitation

Conducting elicitation includes stages that will vary greatly in terms of formality and structure, depending on the approach being used:

- **Introduction:** The introduction sets the stage, sets the pace, and establishes the overall purpose of the elicitation session. This is when the business analysis practitioner sets the tone and establishes rapport with the participants to help ensure effective participation. This initial stage helps get everyone focused and in the right frame of mind by reviewing the subject at hand and the benefits that will be achieved when the objectives are met. During the introduction, it can be helpful to let participants know they will have a chance to confirm elicitation results once the business analysis practitioner consolidates and analyzes the notes to assure that they will be able to review the session notes before they are considered final. This may help participants feel more comfortable and willing to engage.

- **Body:** The body of the elicitation session includes the business analysis practitioner employing their power skills of active listening, reading body language, influencing, empathizing, etc. This is when the primary information is elicited and the objectives of the session are achieved. The transition from the introduction to the body is ideally seamless and participants are unaware as questions become more difficult.

- **Close:** The close occurs at the end of an elicitation session to wrap up the activities and focus on next steps. When the elicitation is done in the form of a workshop, the business analysis practitioner may consider a rundown of the assignment of action items so participants are aware of their responsibilities at the end of the session. When the elicitation session is done in the form of an interview, direction may be provided to interviewees regarding next steps. During the close, the business analysis practitioner should always thank participants for their contributions and time.

Three questions a business analysis practitioner may consider asking at the close of any elicitation session include:

- o Do you have any additional questions?

- o Is there anything we missed or anything we should have talked about but did not?

- o Is there anyone else who might have information that would contribute to the session objectives?

- **Follow-up:** After analyzing and consolidating the information obtained in the session, the business analysis practitioner shares their information to get confirmation from participants that what was captured reflects their intentions. This may be done in a follow-up session or through some other format, depending on stakeholder availability and the amount of information to be confirmed.

Document Elicitation Output

It is important to document the results of elicitation activities, either formally or informally. Documentation can range in formality from user stories to snapshots of whiteboards to fielded information recorded in requirements management tools. The primary documented result is a set of elicitation notes composed of a wealth of information for performing other business analysis tasks. The results may come in the form of sketches, diagrams, models, flip charts, sticky notes, or index cards, to name a few. When the elicitation results are analyzed, the results are documented in the deliverables and forms geared to the audiences who will use them.

Elicitation Techniques

Below are some common elicitation techniques. Using a variety of techniques appeals to different stakeholder styles and ensures a holistic, comprehensive capture of the information needed.

Brainstorming. Brainstorming is a technique used to prompt innovation and creativity by asking groups to consider novel or different solutions. The output generated from the group is often greater than the output from the same group when solutions are recorded individually. By including individuals from various backgrounds or with different perspectives, it becomes possible to consider new ideas and solutions. Brainstorming also increases group cohesion and improves communication within the group.

Collaborative Games. Collaborative games provide a structured way to encourage participation and collaboration when eliciting. Games such as "product box," "fishbowl," and "buy-a-feature" stimulate creative thinking and can be used to elicit priorities and ideas about problems, solutions, and requirements. They may also be used as icebreakers to get better results from elicitation using other techniques. Games have their own rules and typically some type of visual or tactile components. Collaborative games may be used in any environment in which they add value by helping stakeholders work together effectively.

Document Analysis. Information elicited from business, regulatory, and technical documentation is potentially available in many forms. These sources can complement and enrich elicitation obtained through other techniques in which the business analysis practitioner is interacting with others. Some examples of documentation that may be used in eliciting are:

- Business rules and policies,

- Process diagrams,

- Work instructions,

- Data models,

- Software or equipment manuals, and

- Many others.

It is a good practice to identify at least two sources for each topic or question to be explored during elicitation in order to avoid proposing any requirement or solution that is based on the opinion or information from a single source. This is particularly true of written documentation because it is often out of date. That is why business analysis practitioners conduct interviews to confirm the output and documentation resulting from the analysis of the documentation.

Facilitated Workshops. Facilitated workshops are also known as requirements workshops. They are focused sessions that bring key cross-functional stakeholders together to define solution requirements. Workshops are considered a primary technique for quickly defining cross-functional requirements and reconciling stakeholder differences. Due to their interactive-group nature, well-facilitated sessions can also build trust, foster relationships, and improve communication among the participants, which can lead to increased stakeholder consensus.

Focus Groups. A focus group is an elicitation technique that brings together prequalified stakeholders and subject matter experts to learn about their expectations and attitudes toward a proposed product, service, or result. Focus groups are used to gain feedback on completed work or prototypes. Participants are prequalified or prescreened to ensure they meet the desired or targeted representation. Focus groups allow participants to share ideas and build from the feedback that is being shared among the group. It is a great occasion for the business analysis practitioner to watch reactions, facial expressions, and body language, in addition to taking in the information being provided by the group. One drawback of a focus group is that participants may be influenced by group pressure to agree with the stronger-willed participants. The facilitator plays an important role in engaging the entire group to ensure no single participant is demonstrating signs of being influenced by group pressure.

Interviews. An interview is a formal or informal approach to elicit information from stakeholders. It is performed by asking prepared and/or spontaneous questions and documenting the responses. Interviews are often conducted on an individual basis between an interviewer and an interviewee, but may involve multiple interviewers and/or multiple interviewees. Interviewing experienced project participants, stakeholders, and subject matter experts helps identify and define the features and functions of the desired solution. There are two basic types of interviews:

- **Structured interviews** begin with a list of prepared questions with the goal of asking and obtaining answers to every question on the list or within the allotted time.

- **Unstructured interviews** may begin with a list of prepared questions, but the only question that is asked for certain is the first. After that, subsequent questions are based on the answers to the previous questions. The interview takes on a life of its own and requires skill to keep the conversation focused to reach the objective.

Observation. Observation is a technique that provides a direct way of viewing people in their environments to see how they perform their jobs or tasks and carry out processes. It is particularly helpful for detailed processes when people who use the product struggle or are reluctant to articulate their requirements. This type of observation is also called job shadowing. It is usually performed externally by an observer who views a worker performing their job. It can also be performed by a participant observer who performs a process or procedure to experience how it is done to uncover hidden requirements. The objective of the technique is to elicit requirements by observing stakeholders in their work environments. Observation often results in the transfer of a greater amount of unbiased, objective, real information about the problem domain than other forms of elicitation. When asked in a meeting to describe how to go about performing their work, it is probable that a stakeholder may miss steps or under-communicate. Types of observation include:

- **Passive observation**: A business analysis practitioner observes the worker without interrupting, asking questions, or seeking clarification. The observer records what happens, often in the form of a process flow with timings recorded on the diagram. Later, questions may be asked of the worker about the activities observed to clarify and validate notes. An advantage of passive observation is the minimal interruption to the workflow. Some organizations may not allow any other form of observation to be conducted, especially by an outsider. A disadvantage is that the worker may not trust the observer and may perform the work in a nonroutine fashion.

- **Active observation:** This is like passive observation except that the observer interrupts the process or activity, asks questions about what the worker is doing, seeks clarification, asks for opinions, etc. The advantage of active observation is the immediacy of information elicited and the increased amount of information collected. Active observation does, however, interrupt the flow of work, which reduces productivity. It may also change behaviors during the observation.

- **Participatory observation:** In this type of observation, the observer takes part in performing the activities being observed. It allows the observer to generate questions that would never have been thought of otherwise. In addition, the observer has an opportunity to experience what workers are going through when they perform these activities. The observer may discover functions, features, and improvements that don't come up during a facilitated workshop or interview.

- **Simulation**: In this case, the activities, operations, or processes of the work are simulated using a tool that recreates the job duties of the worker. The organization may have training facilities where the observer can interact with test versions of a system or product. With simulation, business analysis practitioners may follow up with the worker through an interview to elicit further details or perform the simulation with the worker.

Prototyping. Prototyping is a method of obtaining early feedback on requirements by providing a model of the expected product before building it. Since prototypes are tangible, stakeholders can experiment with a model of the final product rather than discussing abstract representations of the requirements. Prototypes support the concept of progressive elaboration in iterative cycles of mockup creation, user experimentation, feedback generation, and prototype revision. A prototype can be a mockup of the real result, as in an architectural model, or it can be an early version of the product itself. Elicitation and thorough investigation may not uncover all of the attributes or aspects of a complex solution. Allowing the users and customers to see the product or system as it is being built provides an opportunity for the business to identify issues, clarify requirements, and provide additional information that may have been omitted originally. There are two types of prototypes:

- **Low-fidelity prototype:** Low-fidelity prototypes are completed with a pen and paper, marker and whiteboard, or modeling tool on the computer. Examples of low-fidelity prototypes include:

  o Wireframes,

  o Mockups of interface screens or reports,

  o Architectural renderings of a building,

o   Floor plans,

o   Sketches of a new product, and

o   Any design that is evolving.

A typical use for a low-fidelity prototype is to gather feedback from the intended users by providing a visual representation of what the product/solution will look like and how it will function.

- **High-fidelity prototype:** High-fidelity prototypes create a representation of the final finished product and are usable by the stakeholders who are reviewing them. High-fidelity prototyping is often performed in an iterative fashion. Reviewers can manipulate the screen, enter some data, and move from screen to screen to experience firsthand how the screen will work.

There are two types of high-fidelity prototypes:

o   **Throwaway prototypes** are discarded once the interface has been confirmed. This is like the product prototypes developed by manufacturing companies. The prototype is used to help define the tools and processes for manufacturing the product, but the prototype itself is not used in production.

o   **Evolutionary prototypes** are the actual finished products in the process of being built. The first prototype that is reviewed is the earliest workable version of the final product. With each successive prototyping session, more functionality is added, or the existing functionality is modified to achieve a higher level of quality. In adaptive projects, this is how the product is built. The work is not considered to be a prototype but is an actual slice of the product itself.

Questionnaires and Surveys. Questionnaires and surveys are written sets of questions designed to quickly accumulate information from a large number of respondents. Respondents may represent a diverse population and are often dispersed over a wide geographical area. This method is beneficial for collecting a large amount of information from a large group over a short period of time at a relatively small expense. The outputs are often amenable to quantification, which may provide inputs to decision-making.

Elicitation Definition of Done

Eliciting solution information is an iterative activity of eliciting information and analyzing information. It can be considered a progressive elaboration of information. When information is analyzed, sometimes the quantity decreases because extraneous information is removed. However, when the results are vague and open to interpretation, additional questions need to be asked and more elicitation sessions are then conducted. As the cycle repeats, deeper levels of information detail will be defined and different tools may be required to record the information.

The question of when the elicitation and analysis iterating is done is relatively easy in some environments. In many adaptive environments, for example, these activities iterate until the details are refined enough for the team to identify and estimate the work they need to do to deliver the upcoming product increment.

Knowing when elicitation and analysis iterating is done is a common business analysis quandary in other environments, however. In those situations, the elicitation-analysis cycle continues until the analysis produces no further questions and the information is reduced to a depiction of the solution to the business problem or when the risk of problems emerging from a lack of complete information is acceptable.

The following may indicate when sufficient information has been elicited:

- The stakeholder or problem owner approves the results.
- The model on which the information is based can be completed.
- A dry run or successful prototype is completed.
- The objective has been reached.
- The solution(s) has been identified.
- Stakeholders begin repeating themselves and providing redundant information.
- It takes longer to get answers from the same stakeholders because they are trying to come up with different answers than their previous answers.
- All information pertaining to high-priority requirements has been confirmed by at least two independent sources.

Elicitation Challenges and Responses

There are many challenges associated with elicitation. Some examples and suggestions for meeting those challenges include the following.

Inability to Get Access to the Right Stakeholders. A common issue business analysis practitioners face during the elicitation process is the inability to directly interact with the actual users of the solution. As a result, user interfaces or processes may need to be developed without access to, or input from, those who are directly impacted by the proposed changes.

The business analysis practitioner can address this issue by focusing on the information, not the individual. Sometimes the desired information is available from multiple sources—for example, documentation, training materials, operating procedures, etc. This does present the risk of moving ahead without the right stakeholders, which can lead to solutions that the business never accepts. It is important to advise the sponsor, project manager, and project team when this happens.

In adaptive environments, this challenge is usually mitigated with the inclusion of a customer representative on the team to whom those building the product have easy access.

Conflicting Viewpoints and Needs among Different Stakeholders. Considering that stakeholders typically come from different parts of the organization with their own pain points and experiences, it is not surprising that they often disagree about what they need or the solution to that need. Rapport with stakeholders and a healthy dose of empathy will assist in understanding various points of view and helping stakeholders understand one another. Staying focused on the business problem being addressed and the benefits to stakeholders will also help. Recognizing that change is threatening to many can mitigate frustration when stakeholders obstruct progress. Maintaining neutrality as the trusted adviser and providing clarity around when and to whom decisions should be escalated will also help navigate impasses caused by conflicting opinions.

In adaptive environments, this challenge is usually mitigated with the inclusion of a customer representative on the team who makes decisions on behalf of the stakeholders.

Not Getting the Requirements Needed. Sometimes stakeholders struggle to understand the business problem they are trying to solve, or they approach elicitation activities with a solution in mind. In either instance, stakeholders' abilities to define what they want and need may be compromised.

To address these challenges, the business analysis practitioner should ask stakeholders for help in understanding the problem domain and focus their attention on the problem or opportunity they wish to address. After clarifying the situation, the discussion should be focused on the high-level requirements. When the business analysis practitioner helps to break down the high-level requirements and walks the stakeholders through the process, the stakeholders will be prevented from moving directly to the solution. When it becomes difficult to elicit needs and high-level requirements from the stakeholders, the business analysis practitioner needs to continue asking clarifying questions to draw out the requirements.

Stakeholders Do Not Know What They Want. Sometimes the problem is understood, but the stakeholders cannot see themselves in the context of the solution. To address this challenge, using techniques such as prototyping or storyboards often helps stakeholders visualize each of the possible solutions. Working iteratively and/or incrementally to get feedback before developing an entire solution can also address this challenge by giving stakeholders something to respond to rather than having to imagine what might address their needs.

Stakeholders Not Providing Sufficient Detail to Develop the Solution. Stakeholders may not have experience providing requirements or may not understand business analysis or the business analyst role. Sometimes stakeholders are unaware of the level of detail required or they cannot figure out how to go about describing such details.

Eliciting requirements using visual modeling techniques often helps address this issue. Engaging stakeholders in modeling can open dialogue that may not be possible through interview questions, surveys, or straight discussion. Engaging stakeholders to collaborate on a workflow, or to assist with breaking down a problem into a hierarchical model, can help get the details needed. Turning elicitation into a visual or tactical exercise focuses the stakeholder on completing the visual or physical elements, resulting in discovery of details that might not be possible to obtain without the imagery and participation.

Case Study: Elicit Solution Information

George is working on the home remodeling project and needs to elicit ideas from current homeowners. He conducts a *survey* to obtain initial information from them about what they like and do not like about the features of their homes.

With input from the team, George develops a survey with closed-ended questions and an optional, open-ended question at the end for additional comments. The survey is made available online to everyone who lives in the homes and is optionally distributed by mail with a self-addressed, stamped envelope for ease of returning. Considering the value of the home remodel that residents may receive, George expects a high response rate. Some of the topics from the survey appear in Table 4-1.

After the survey closes, George facilitates a *focus group* of homeowners who were among the first cohort of residents in the homes. The goal of the focus group is to dig deeper into what modifications the homeowners and their families would value most. Specifically, he wants to see and hear their reactions to changes the team is considering after receiving the survey feedback.

The following questions are asked in the focus group:

- What is the best experience your family has had in your home?

- How do you feel about your home when someone new comes to visit?

Table 4-1. Survey Results for Existing Homeowners

Our kitchen works well for the way my family prepares meals.			
Strongly Disagree	Somewhat Disagree	Somewhat Agree	Strongly Agree
81%	14%	3%	2%

My home works well when people are working from home or need private space.			
Strongly Disagree	Somewhat Disagree	Somewhat Agree	Strongly Agree
68%	17%	9%	6%

I value the sustainability and eco-friendly elements of my home.			
Strongly Disagree	Somewhat Disagree	Somewhat Agree	Strongly Agree
1%	4%	11%	84%

My home is easy for everyone to move around and get to where they need to go.			
Strongly Disagree	Somewhat Disagree	Somewhat Agree	Strongly Agree
28%	38%	19%	15%

The exterior of my home is appealing.			
Strongly Disagree	Somewhat Disagree	Somewhat Agree	Strongly Agree
6%	8%	52%	34%

- If you could change one thing in your home, what would it be?

- What comes to mind when you think of cooking in your kitchen?

- What are the biggest challenges your family experiences related to layout or design?

- Is there anything else about your home that you think would be helpful for us to hear?

The focus group results yielded stakeholder requirements, including:

- Residents should be able to easily move around all spaces on the first floor using a walker, wheelchair, or other mobility aid.

- Residents of any ability should be able to participate together in family meal preparation, whether standing up or sitting down.

- Residents should be able to easily close off one to two spaces in the home to create temporary privacy for working or resting.

George uses the information from the focus group and the stakeholder requirements identified as the starting point for a requirements workshop that he facilitates with leads from SCC sales and marketing, architecture, and construction. At the end of the workshop, many solution requirements are captured.

To manage the product scope and ensure that requirements add value, George and his team use a *requirements traceability matrix* per the plan (see Table 4-2). He adds the stakeholder and solution requirements to the requirements traceability matrix, along with columns for the requirements attributes that were agreed to during planning.

(Continued)

Table 4-2. Requirements Traceability Matrix for Case Study

ID	Requirement	Status	Priority	Source	Objectives	Author
SR.1	Residents of any ability will be able to participate together in family meal preparation, whether standing up or sitting down.				BO3 PO3	George
FR.1.1	Work surfaces along walls will be able to be hidden behind counters.	E	M	Focus group (date)	BO3 PO3	George
FR.1.2	Workspace counters will be height-adjustable to allow people of different heights to work safely.	E	M	Focus group (date)	BO3 PO3	George
NFR.1.1	Kitchen will accommodate 6 to 8 people of different abilities working together for meal preparation.	E	M	Focus group (date)	BO3 PO3	George
NFR.1.2	Height-adjustable workspace counters will be able to support 150 lbs. (70 kg).	E	M	Focus group (date)	BO3 PO3	George
SR.2	Residents of all abilities will be able to easily use all facilities in the home.				BO3 PO3	George
FR.2.1	Sinks will be height-adjustable.	E	M	Workshop (date)	BO3 PO3	George
NFR.2.1	Doorways will accommodate all standard mobility assistance devices, including walkers, wheelchairs, and scooters.	E	M	BRule02	BO3 PO3	George

Key:

Requirements:	Status options:	Priority (MoSCoW):	Objectives:
SR = Stakeholder requirement	E = Elicited	M = Must have	BO = Business objective
FR = Functional requirement	A = Approved	S = Should have	PO = Project objective
NFR = Nonfunctional requirement	I = In progress	C = Could have	
	C = Completed	W = Won't have	
	X = Canceled		
	R = Rejected		
	D = Deferred		
	P = Implemented		

Rani works closely with the product owner on her team to identify requirements for the IoT smart home project. She facilitates a workshop with the product owner and team members from sales and marketing, IT, and architecture, as well as the project manager. The product manager serves as the scribe in the workshop.

In the workshop, Rani begins with a brainstorming exercise using the *product tree* technique (see Figure 4-1) to identify the potential smart home features.

Following the product tree workshop, Rani and the product owner explore options for prioritizing the features. They decide to invite a current homeowner, a potential first-time homebuyer, and the sponsor to a prioritization workshop using *buy-a-feature*. Rani gives the product owner and other stakeholders the same amount of play money and they are invited to "spend" it on the features they would like to have in the home.

Based on the results of the buy-a-feature game (see Table 4-3), Rani and the team prioritize the features and modify the product backlog accordingly. The features are prioritized from highest to lowest, according to how much was spent on them.

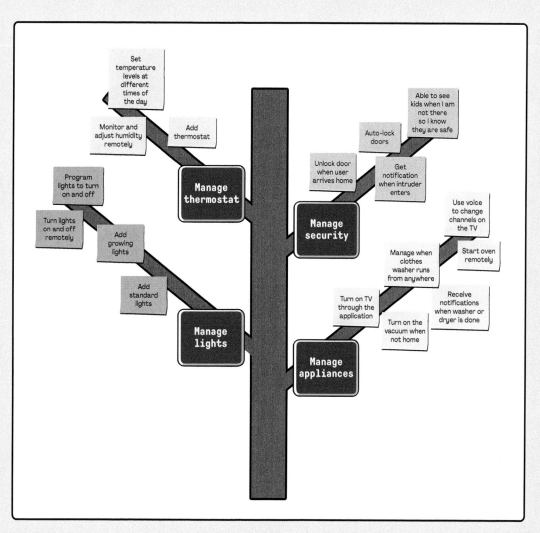

Figure 4-1. Product Tree Brainstorming Exercise

Table 4-3. Buy-a-Feature Game to Prioritize the Product Backlog

	Product Owner	Current Homeowner	First-Time Homebuyer	Sponsor	Total
Voice-activated blinds	$40	$35	$25		$100
Alerts when laundry is finished		$25		$25	$50
Unlocks door when user arrives home			$30	$50	$80
Controls lights remotely	$10		$20		$30
Voice-activated lights	$50	$40	$25	$25	$140

Analyze Solution Information

Using a business analysis mindset helps when analyzing input from elicitation. Thinking holistically and comprehensively, while sticking to the need, assists in decomposing and then organizing inputs into coherent categories before seeking to relate the pieces.

Overview

Analysis is everything the business analysis practitioner does to close the gaps in understanding the solution. This is the fundamental piece of the business analysis practitioner's work and is as much a creative process as it is a rigorous endeavor. It includes the activities that earn business analysis practitioners their reputations as being detail-oriented, which involves examining, breaking down, and synthesizing information to further understand, complete, and improve analysis. It involves progressively and iteratively working through information to more granular levels of detail and often entails abstracting to a higher level of detail. Analysis provides structure to the requirements and related solution information.

Analysis and elicitation are done iteratively—what is elicited gets analyzed, which leads to more elicitation. Any solution information that is elicited may be analyzed, including the following: business, stakeholder, solution or transition requirements, models, assumptions, constraints, issues, risks, acceptance criteria, and business rules.

Central to analysis is modeling. A model is a structured representation of information and may include text, tables, or diagrams. Much analysis entails using models to identify and refine aspects of the solution, particularly requirements, and how they relate to one another. Business analysis practitioners apply various models, depending on variables, such as how much is known, the model objective, the audience, the stakeholder needs, past experience, and organizational good practices.

Model types, and examples of each, include:

- **Scope models.** Includes context diagram, use case diagram, and SWOT (strengths, weaknesses, opportunities, threats) diagram.

- **Process models.** Includes process flow, use case, and user story.

- **Rule models.** Includes business rules catalog, decision tree, and decision table.

- **Data models.** Includes entity relationship diagram, data dictionary, and data flow diagram.

- **Interface models.** Includes user interface flow, wireframes, and display-action-response.

Any type of information might nourish analysis, such as stakeholder categories, problem and solution scope, identified business rules, technological constraints, and stakeholder concerns and assumptions. Analysis can provide a structure that allows prioritization, helps discover dependencies, and assists in evaluating the impact of changes and risks.

Product owners in adaptive environments may partner with the business analysis practitioner for analysis of solution information, particularly when it comes to modeling. Product owners may not be familiar with many of the modeling techniques available, so the business analysis practitioner can advocate for the use of various models, as well as facilitate the collaboration of the product owner, team members, and other stakeholders in the exploration of solution details using the models.

Value of Analyzing Solution Information

The value of analysis is realized through the iterative nature of the process of elicitation. Analysis is how the business analysis practitioner is able to confirm the intention of the stakeholders as expressed in elicitation. Analysis ultimately provides the development team with what they need to produce the solution, whether it be software or widgets. The business analysis practitioner asks questions in different ways, presents options and examples to inspire feedback, and collaborates with stakeholders to refine provided information. Analysis makes requirements actionable.

Modeling, a cornerstone of analysis, concisely conveys large amounts of information, which makes it enormously valuable to the business analysis practitioner. The visual nature of models helps communicate complexity. For example, most people have an easier time understanding how an application interface will work if they can see a picture of what it looks like. Use cases, as another example, make it easier than simple text to identify functional requirements that specify the interaction between a user and a system.

As solution information is refined, new models are produced, which serve to structure the requirements. Using various traceability strategies, the requirements either reference the models or are referenced in the models. For example, the requirements traceability matrix is a model that can be used to allocate requirements to the solution components or project phases, thus ensuring the completeness of the delivery. It may also trace requirements to test cases or design documents, which helps structure the testing plan and reveals gaps in solution information. Tracing solution requirements to stakeholder and business requirements helps manage scope and validate that requirements add value.

How to Analyze Solution Information

Business analysis practitioners begin analyzing solution information as soon as there is information about a solution or potential solution to analyze. During Business Value Assessment, and prior to chartering an initiative, a business analysis practitioner conducts analysis and may generate models, such as capability tables, to identify potential solutions to a business need. Business, stakeholder, and high-level solution requirements may be identified, decomposed, modeled, clarified, and otherwise analyzed. Business analysis practitioners do only what is required for the decision makers to make well-informed decisions. Once the solution is identified and the initiative chartered, the business analysis practitioner models and generates additional details about the solution until assumptions are addressed and gaps in understanding are filled.

Case Study: Analyze Solution Information

The requirements for the house continue to evolve as the business analysis team iteratively elicits and analyzes the requirements. As they are refined, George recognizes that the acceptance criteria need to be defined. He works with the team and customers to elicit them and updates the *requirements traceability matrix to* include the *acceptance criteria* (see Table 4-4).

Table 4-4. Requirements Traceability Matrix with Acceptance Criteria

ID	Requirement	Status	Priority	Objectives	Author	Acceptance Criteria	Model Area
SR.1	Residents of any ability will be able to participate together in family meal preparation whether standing up or sitting down.			BO3 PO3	George		
FR.1.1	Work surfaces along walls will be able to be hidden behind counters.	E	M	BO3 PO3	George	When the counter is hidden: • There is no evidence of the counter. • Floor space can be used for other activities.	Area 1
FR.1.2	Workspace counters will be height-adjustable to allow people of different heights to work safely.	E	M	BO3 PO3	George	The counter can be set at any height between 2 ft. and 4 ft. (60–122 cm).	Area 1
NFR.1.1	The kitchen will accommodate 6 to 8 people of different abilities working together for meal preparation.	E	M	BO3 PO3	George	Eight people can be in the kitchen preparing food with a minimum of 1 ft. (30.5 cm) of space on either side of each person.	Area 1
NFR.1.2	Height-adjustable workspace counters will be able to support 150 lbs. (70 kg).	E	M	BO3 PO3	George	The counter can hold the weight of 150 lbs. (70 kg) of kitchenware for 7 days.	Area 1

Based on the requirements, George collaborates with the team to develop a low-fidelity model (see Figure 4-2) that traces requirements to various areas of the model.

The model reflects the stakeholder and functional requirements, resulting in key aspects of solution design. They are careful not to identify how the requirements will be delivered technically (using springs, hinges, etc.) as it is their job, as business analysis practitioners, to refrain from identifying technical design.

The process of getting the design refined enough for approval involves multiple rounds of updates, validation from stakeholders that the design reflects their intentions, and revisions based on stakeholder feedback.

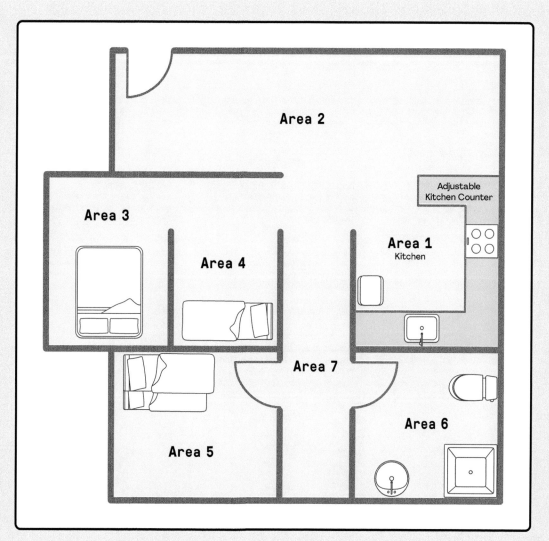

Figure 4-2. Numbered Areas of Smart Home

Based on what is elicited in the product tree workshop, Rani and the team identify a theme and epics for the smart home's IoT application (see Table 4-5). She and the team slice the epics into user stories to facilitate development. They continue the traceability of the solution requirements by adding acceptance criteria to the user stories (see Table 4-5). Rani and her team collaborate with the product owner on these activities and getting the product backlog items added to the product backlog. They expect to do further refinement as the stories get prioritized and closer to development.

As George and Rani refine their requirements, they learn about *business rules* (see Table 4-6) they need to be aware of, which will impact the solution requirements. They also collaborate with their teams and customers to identify nonfunctional requirements.

(Continued)

Table 4-5. Sample Themes, Epics, and User Stories for Building a Smart Home

Theme—Introduce a Smart Home Application		
Epics		
As a smart home owner, I want to manage and monitor my home security, so that I am able to protect my property and family.	As a smart home owner, I want to manage and monitor my home environment so the people in the home are comfortable.	As a smart home owner, I want to manage and monitor my home appliances, so that I am able to easily use them.
User Stories		
As Henry, the homeowner, I want to be able to see what my children are doing in the home when I am not there, so I know they are safe.	As a smart home owner, I want to be able to set the temperature to different levels at different times of the day to save energy.	As Henry, the homeowner, I want to manage the clothes washer to run at any time, so I can use it outside of peak energy hours.
As a smart home owner, I want to be notified when someone enters my home when I am not there, so I know if there is an intruder.	As Sara, the homeowner, I want to be able to remotely monitor and adjust the humidity level in my home, so I can protect my plants.	As a smart home owner, I want to be able to run the vacuum when I am not home, so that my house is clean when I get home.
Acceptance Criteria		
Given that I am not in my home, and I am not expecting others to be there, when someone enters, an alert is sent to my phone notifying me.	Given that the home environment IoT system is up and running, when I am not at home, I am able to adjust the humidity level in my home.	Given that the appliance IoT system is up and running, when I am not home, I am able to operate the vacuum, including: • Start • Stop • Pause • Empty container

Table 4-6. Rules and Requirements That Impact Solution Requirements

Business Rules
BRule01. Customer must be a registered user to receive support.
BRule02. All SSC structures will adhere to ADA or local regulatory guidelines for accessibility.
BRule03. Support calls beyond the number allowed in the service package purchased will be billed at US$50 per call.

Nonfunctional Requirements
1. System allows for 1,000 devices.
2. System application will run on mobile devices and personal computers with one of the following operating systems: Android 5.0 and higher, iOS 9.0 and higher, OS X 10.10 and higher, and Windows 10 or higher.
3. Changes to system settings will be in effect within 1 minute of saving changes.

Story Mapping

Rani facilitates *story mapping* with the team to arrange the user stories in the order they will likely be developed and released to customers (see Figure 4-3). This technique supports a product team with release allocation, where features or product components are assigned to different product releases. This also helps Rani facilitate prioritization with the product owner.

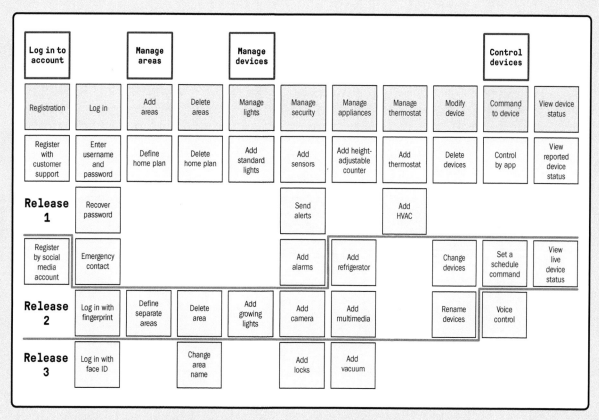

Figure 4-3. Story Mapping Example

Rani facilitates a session with the team, including the product owner, to come up with a low-fidelity wireframe for the smart home's IoT application. The user interface/user experience (UI/UX) team members then create a high-fidelity *wireframe* using the tools they plan to use for development (see Figure 4-4).

(Continued)

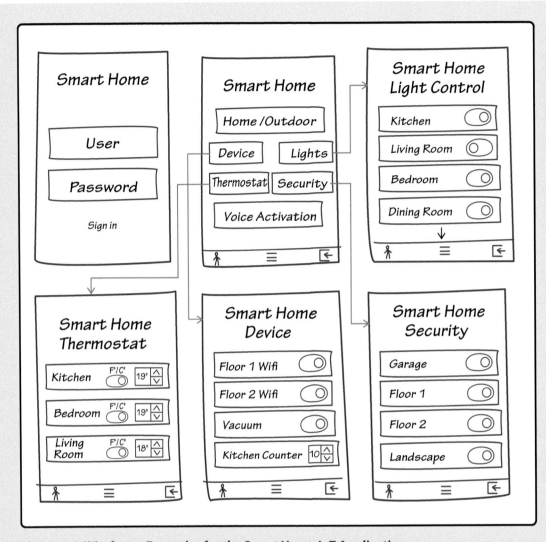

Figure 4-4. Wireframe Examples for the Smart Home IoT Application

Requirements Dependencies

Even though their projects entail two distinct efforts, George makes sure to meet with Rani to go over the model that his team develops so Rani is able to see the home where her IoT solution will be installed. Rani suggests adding voice-activated, height-adjustable counters to the IoT smart home functionality. George conducts an impact analysis using the requirements traceability matrix to confirm that the suggestion supports the business and project objectives (it is an important safety feature), and to understand any impact it would have on other requirements or aspects of the solution. He then presents the requirement to the customer to get their decision on whether to include it, which they decide to do (see Figure 4-5).

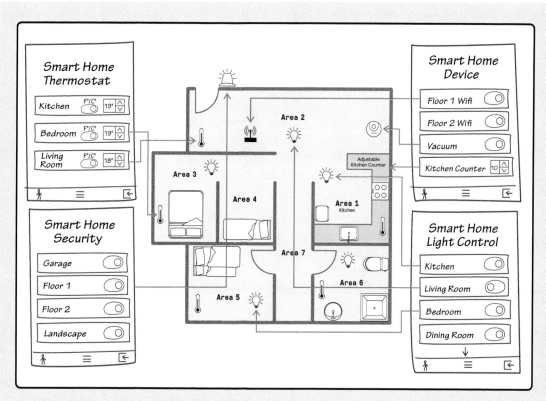

Figure 4-5. Smart Home IoT Application

As changes occur throughout the initiative, George uses the requirements traceability matrix to identify impacts.

Package Solution Information

```
Using a business analysis mindset promotes a holistic perspective
regarding who may need to understand or use the results of business
analysis work. It also enhances creativity when communicating the
outputs generated by business analysis work with stakeholders, so they
can easily understand the outputs and respond to them with feedback,
decisions, or other responses that add value to the solution.
```

Overview

Throughout business analysis activities, much information is created, collected, and shared. Solution information, including requirements, can include different types or levels of detail. Requirements may refer to business or stakeholder requirements, and issues might be stakeholder issues or product defects. Solution information takes on different states as various processes or activities consume and produce the information. At different points in business analysis work, requirements can be in a verified, validated, prioritized, or approved state. Further, the solution information may be stored in a variety of forms, such as tools, documents, notes, emails, and people's minds.

Packaging solution information is the work of assembling the information that will be of value to stakeholders and making it consumable so they can use it as needed, such as further refining the information, making a decision, validating or verifying requirements, or developing the solution.

For example, a requirements workshop may yield solution information, including functional requirements of a product, models, business rules, user stories, acceptance criteria, nonfunctional requirements, issues, risks, status, or constraints. The output of that workshop may include screenshots of whiteboards, sticky notes on a wall, parking lot items in a spreadsheet, or other items. Packaging may result in a business requirements document, so someone can review and approve the requirements; a requirements traceability matrix, so it is possible for the business analysis team to confirm coverage of requirements; or updated user stories on a product backlog to enable the product owner to prioritize them.

The needs of various audiences are taken into consideration, and not every solution detail that is elicited needs to be packaged. For example, if an interview reveals information that, when confirmed with other sources, is identified as out of scope and therefore not to be considered for the solution, the information may be retained by the business analysis practitioner but not necessarily packaged for stakeholders, since it will not be used by them.

Value of Packaging Solution Information

The outputs of efforts to define and refine the solution may be in a format that makes sense to the individuals involved in the creation of that output, but not in a format that is consumable or usable to the stakeholders who receive the information. Packaging solution information is an ongoing activity that facilitates a shared understanding of the solution and related information at any given time. As solution information is progressively elaborated, stakeholders are able to understand emerging details and use them for some purpose that adds value to the solution and supports the business analysis work. The information package should be clear, concise, and usable for the stakeholders.

How to Package Solution Information

After obtaining details about the solution, whether through impromptu conversations, scheduled workshops, or other methods, the business analysis practitioner assesses how the information needs to be used and packages that information in a format suitable for the objectives of the stakeholders who will be using the information at that time. A significant component of the solution information is the requirements. Documented requirements may be referred to as solution documentation, which could be any one of the following or a combination of more than one:

- Requirements specification (common, generic term referring to all documents that contain requirements), including but not limited to the following:

    o Business requirements document (BRD)

    o Functional requirements specification

    o Software requirements specification

- Collection of written user stories,

- Set of use cases with related nonfunctional requirements, and

- List of items on a backlog.

Considerations when packaging solution information include when the information is being assembled, the intended audience, and how they will use it. Below are a few examples of packaging solution information.

Business Requirements Document

The format for a business requirements document (BRD) should be agreed upon in planning and the creation of the document may be done as soon as there are requirements to capture. The audience for this document includes the business stakeholders who review, validate, and approve the solution documentation. The team developing the solution also consumes the information in the BRD and is heavily dependent on it, because it serves as the blueprint for the solution they are being asked to build. When development work is outsourced, it is essential for the solution documentation to be precise and detailed because the outsourced team often lacks the business knowledge that an internal development team has (see Figure 4-6).

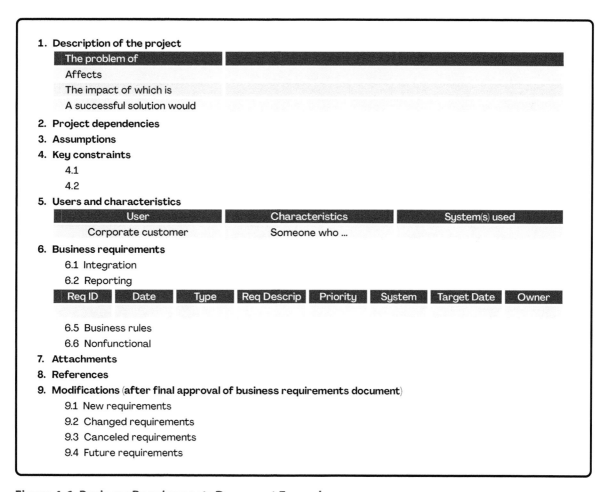

Figure 4-6. Business Requirements Document Example

Requirements Traceability Matrix

A requirements traceability matrix (RTM) is a grid that links product requirements from their origin to the deliverables that satisfy them. The format for an RTM—and who will be permitted to update it—should be agreed upon in planning. Populating the document may be done as soon as there are requirements to trace. Traceability matrices typically include the requirements' status, sources, relationships (including dependencies), and other information to provide evidence that the requirements are delivered as stated. Tracing may be done at the individual requirement level, at a group level, or at the feature or function level.

Factors for selecting the level to trace requirements to include:

- The amount of time available to trace,

- The kind of solution being developed,

- Associated regulations that may impact tracing, and

- Organizational practices and preferences.

Sometimes the details in the traceability matrix are such that it becomes the primary requirements documentation. In those cases, the business stakeholders, solution development team, and others will use the matrix to review, validate, and approve the solution documentation like they would a business requirements document (see Figure 4-7). The business analysis practitioner uses it for many reasons, including:

- Communicating with stakeholders regarding status and other information of interest;

- Conducting an impact analysis to determine how a change in one requirement impacts other requirements, artifacts, or deliverables;

- Ensuring that solution requirements are in scope by tracing them back to the business requirements; and

- Ensuring that there is coverage for requirements, such as test cases, design documents, models, etc.

	A	B	C	D	E	F	G	H	I
1	REQUIREMENTS TRACEABILITY MATRIX								
2	Project Name:		\<optional\>						
3	Cost Center:		\<required\>						
4	Project Description:		\<required\>						
5	ID	Associate ID	Requirements Description	Business Needs, Opportunities, Goals, Objectives	Project Objectives	WBS Deliverables	Product Design	Product Development	Test Cases
6		1.0							
7	001	1.1							
8		1.2							
9		1.2.1							
10		2.0							
11	002	2.1							
12		2.1.1							
13		3.0							
14	003	3.1							
15		3.2							
16	004	4.0							
17	005	5.0							

Figure 4-7. Requirements Traceability Matrix Example

Product Backlog

The product backlog contains ordered product backlog items, typically expressed as user stories representing stakeholder requirements. User story documentation is informal—just enough to support their development within the iteration selected for story development. User stories often subscribe to a format that includes an actor, a goal, and a motivation or statement of the value to be delivered. The product backlog can also contain business rules, nonfunctional requirements, and other solution information that may be included in user story acceptance criteria, posted on the product backlog, or however the team decides to maintain awareness of them. Approval for what is on the product backlog and the ordering of the product backlog items is the responsibility of the product owner who makes those decisions. Given the transparent nature of adaptive environments, the product backlog is available for viewing by anyone who is interested at any time.

The product backlog can include product backlog items at any point they are identified, including as soon as the solution is initially identified in the business value assessment (see Figure 4-8).

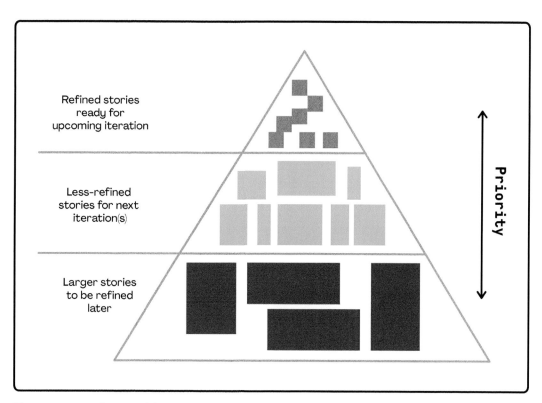

Figure 4-8. Product Backlog Example

Case Study: Package Solution Information

Throughout the project, George and Rani package solution information in a variety of formats, including a product roadmap, story map, and other tool outputs, depending on stakeholder needs. George uses what was decided on during planning to guide what he includes. He revises the outputs as needed to make them easy for stakeholders to understand, such as avoiding acronyms, identifying all parts of any images or models with legends, and steering clear of technical language.

After putting the package together, George validates the information by retracing the requirements in the requirements traceability matrix to the business and project objectives. Information is verified during a walk-through with other business analysis practitioners and key team members, which George facilitates. Once validated and verified, approval is obtained by getting email approvals from the project manager, construction lead, and sales and marketing lead, and a signature from the sponsor per the responsibility assignment matrix defined in governance planning.

Rani's solution information is captured in the backlog, and validation and verification are accomplished through backlog refinement. Rani and her team create a checklist for their definition of ready (DoR) for the user stories to indicate when the stories are ready to be pulled into the iteration for development (see Figure 4-9). As the DoR is met for the user stories of highest priority, the team pulls them into their planning session for the next iteration to define the tasks for completing the work.

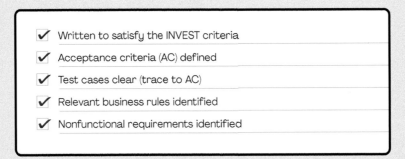

Figure 4-9. User Story "Definition of Ready" Checklist

George and Rani collaborate throughout these activities to identify any impacts of changes to each other's initiatives.

Organizational Transition and Solution Evaluation Domain

Introduction

Organizational Transition and Solution Evaluation involves a business analysis practitioner preparing the organization for a smooth, effective organizational transition. This builds confidence that the organization is ready to adopt the solution (or partial solution) and that the solution will generate the intended business value and be sustained during operation.

By doing this work and eliciting, analyzing, and providing sufficient information, the organization demonstrates it is not only able to make the change, but is also prepared to use, measure, and sustain the solution while realizing the value of the solution as expressed in the business case.

What to Expect in This Domain

This domain offers an approach for managing the organizational transition activities and evaluation of the solution.

Organizational Transition and Solution Evaluation consists of three key practices to help the business analysis practitioner enable the organization for transition and ensure its business value will be realized and sustained after the release of the solution (see Figure 5-1).

- **Enable Organizational Transition** allows the organization to integrate the solution, or part of the solution, into its operations by tracking all transition requirements and activities; assessing organizational readiness for transition; identifying gaps, issues, and risks; and taking the necessary actions.

- **Facilitate Go/No-Go Decision** facilitates the go/no-go decision for the key stakeholders accountable for the solution by analyzing all important aspects of the solution and impact to the organization and presenting the results to them so they can make the best decision.

- **Evaluate Solution Performance** activities are carried out to determine how well an implemented solution, or part of an implemented solution, meets the business value proposition as articulated in the business case.

These practices appear as separate practices done independently, but they may be performed seamlessly in some environments, particularly those using an adaptive approach, in which product increments are being implemented frequently and regularly.

In other environments, these practices occur at different times during the product life cycle. Enable Organizational Transition occurs prior to the release of the solution. It can start during the development of the solution and continue until the time of its release. To release the solution, stakeholders review the result of the analysis to make a go/no-go decision. The business analysis practitioner facilitates all these activities. Finally, after the release, the organization evaluates the solution to determine if the expected business value of the solution has been achieved.

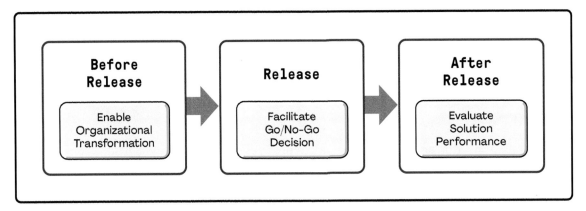

Figure 5-1. The Three Practices in Organizational Transition and Solution Evaluation

Main Benefits of the Practices in This Domain

A successful organizational transition practice gives the organization the knowledge and assurance that the solution will be accepted and sustained by the organization when a release decision is made. It can also save the organization's reputation by minimizing the risk of "go fever" and avoiding a potentially high-profile failure due to a rush to launch a solution for which the organization was not prepared.

The "go fever" results from both individual and collective aspects of human behavior. It stems from the tendency of individuals to become overly committed to a previously chosen course of action because of the time and resources already expended, despite the fact that future benefits could be small or insufficient, or worse still, significant risks could be introduced.

Successful product releases depend on delivering the solution with its expected capabilities and preparing the people who are going to use it.

Solution evaluation consists of the work done to analyze measurements obtained by comparing the actual results of solution performance to the expected or desired values, as defined by the solution evaluation criteria.

These activities may reveal opportunities or problems with the solution that trigger business value assessment activities to find ways to refine the solution or justification to retire a solution.

Key Questions Answered in This Domain

- What needs to be done before organizational transition?
- How can the organizational willingness and ability to accept change be assessed?
- What is the transition strategy and how to transition from the current state to the future state?
- Who is accountable for the solution and has decision-making authority?
- How can stakeholder approval for the solution release be obtained?
- Does the solution produce the intended business value?
- How, who, and when to measure solution performance?

Enable Organizational Transition

The business analysis mindset is open to identifying, prioritizing, and addressing stakeholders' areas of concerns while enabling organizational transition. Thinking systemically, the business analysis practitioner promotes confidence about the organizational readiness to adopt and accept the solution outcomes.

Overview

Enable Organizational Transition is a group of activities performed to build confidence that the organization is ready for the transition, and to demonstrate how the organization will transition from the current state to the future state by integrating the solution or partial solution into its operations.

Transition requirements describe temporary capabilities, such as data conversion, training requirements, and operational changes, needed to transition from the current state. Transition requirements may also be discovered during modeling, definition, and elaboration of product requirements as the solution is refined, as well as during transition preparation.

During this practice, the business analysis practitioner prepares and follows the transition approach in a systematic, disciplined review to ensure that all transition requirements and related activities are completed, which includes required communications, training, procedural updates, data conversion, and all documentation necessary for a successful transition.

The business analysis practitioner conducts a readiness assessment based on the readiness assessment plan to verify that the transition requirements have been met prior to release. During the readiness assessment, some gaps may be identified that need to be addressed through corrective actions. The business analysis practitioner may conduct another readiness assessment to ensure the organization is adequately prepared. These iterative readiness assessments confirm that the organization, team, process, system, and product are prepared for the transition and operation of the solution.

The business analysis practitioner tracks activities associated with the organizational transition, based on the schedule established in the transition plan, which include but are not limited to:

- Identify, utilize, and address all transition requirements, including development of communications, time lines, training, procedure updates, recovery plans, and other collateral needed to successfully transition and adapt to the future state.

- Plan what, who, and how to communicate the results of transition activities and decisions.

- Plan how to transition by analyzing, recommending, and getting approval for the transition strategy.

- Identify the decision makers and decision criteria regarding whether to deploy all of the solution, part of the solution, or none at all.

- Develop a time line of transition activities, including deadlines for completion of milestones. In its most formal format, the time line should have a prescribed schedule that is developed in collaboration with—and managed by—those responsible for project management and operations.

- Identify and analyze any additional risks while transitioning the solution.

- Implement organizational transition risk responses.

- Coordinate the transition with other releases that are part of enabling the future state, and with those that are independent of the solution being deployed. This will ensure that implementation occurs at a time when the organization can integrate the changes, including disruptions caused by the transition itself, and that the rollout does not conflict with other ongoing programs and projects.

- Complete all required training materials and delivery of training.

- Complete or update organizational procedures and relevant working aids and create a reference guide for the organization.

- Purchase licenses and install the required hardware and software needed to support the solution.

- Coordinate other activities within the organization to ensure that the implementation occurs at a time when the organization can integrate the changes and that the rollout does not conflict with other ongoing programs and projects.

- Conduct the readiness assessment based on the solution readiness plan to find the gaps.

- Address deficiencies identified in the organizational readiness assessment.

- Ensure any disruption to business operations is clearly identified, communicated, and accepted by customers.

- Communicate the results of transition activities and decisions to the stakeholders identified in the transition plan.

- Refine and adopt the transition strategy based on the organizational readiness.

Value of Enabling Organizational Transition

This practice enables the organization and stakeholders to smoothly and effectively transition to the desired state to minimize resistance and mitigate risk. It increases the success of the solution by ensuring that affected individuals and groups are ready to adopt the required changes. It also creates a shared understanding of what needs to be done to transition to the future state and ensure transition requirements will be met.

This practice also ensures the organization successfully embraces the changes resulting from the implementation of the new solution or solution component, and that all product components or overall benefits expected from the solution can be sustained after go-live.

Enable Organizational Transition:

- Helps ensure a smooth transition;

- Helps identify and mitigate risks;

- Increases operational efficiency; and

- Builds trust in the organization, the team, and the process.

How to Enable Organizational Transition

To prepare for the organizational transition, the business analysis practitioner uses a variety of methods, such as brainstorming, facilitated workshops, and interviews, to acquire the necessary data and information. The business analysis practitioner uses this information to develop a transition approach, which includes a transition plan (planning transition activities), transition strategy, and readiness assessment plan.

The business analysis practitioner tracks the implementation of the transition activities based on the transition approach. To ensure successful implementation of activities and build confidence in the organization, the business analysis practitioner conducts a readiness assessment to identify gaps, risks, or issues that have not yet been addressed.

Based on the results, the business analysis practitioner identifies further activities and transition requirements to address the gaps, issues, and risks as well as refine the transition plan, transition strategy, and readiness assessment plan. This is done iteratively until no more gaps are found or the remaining risks are acceptable and the organization has met all requirements (see Figure 5-2).

Some examples of the gaps, risks, or issues may include:

- Lack of training,

- Risk of conversion failure due to incorrect conversion strategy,

- Incomplete data conversion,

- Lack of procedures, and

- Lack of coordination.

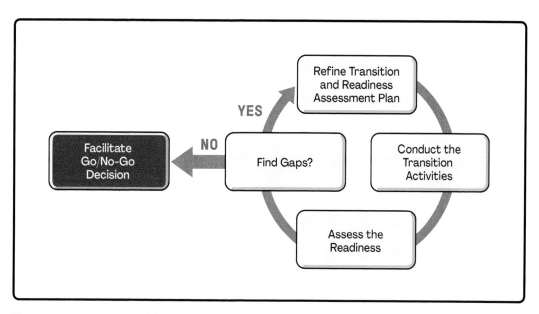

Figure 5-2. Steps to Enabling the Organizational Transition

To enable organizational transition, the business analysis practitioner uses a variety of methods such as:

- Facilitated workshops and interviews to identify any gaps in organizational readiness;

- Process flows, created to describe the transition processes, making it easier for those responsible for the transition to know what needs to be done; and

- Audits, risk assessments, facilitated workshops, and interviews used for the assessment.

The following are artifacts produced when enabling the organizational transition:

- **Transition approach.** The transition approach includes a transition plan (planning transition activities), transition strategy, and readiness assessment plan. The transition approach takes into account known transition considerations and readiness factors to plan the transition schedule. The approach also identifies which stakeholders should be involved in preparing for the transition and how best to collaborate with them. Without the involvement of key stakeholders in transition activities, the transition work will be poorly executed.

- **Transition plan.** The transition plan includes the tasks that need to be completed before the go-live date, the expected completion dates, and the resources required, and shows the sequence/dependency of the tasks. A transition plan is based on a readiness assessment and chosen transition strategy.

  From a business analysis perspective, a transition plan includes actionable and measurable transition requirements. While there are generic aspects of transition plans that can be repeated from solution to solution, other aspects are highly focused on the products and industries impacted by the transition, as well as the specific organization in which the transition is taking place.

  Insights gained from analysis of the existing solution, the successor solution (some other initiatives that depend on this solution), and the transition requirements are used to define the transition activities. A responsibility assignment matrix can be used to identify who has a role to approve or sign off on the solution.

- **Transition strategy.** Selection of the best transition strategy is an essential part of the transition approach. An incorrect strategy selection and implementation creates risks and can result in a failure.

  There are several strategies for solution deployment. These strategies apply equally to automated, manual, and mixed solutions. Commonly used strategies for planning a transition include:

  o *Massive, one-time cutover*. A massive, one-time cutover occurs prior to installing the replacement and phasing out the prior system.

  o *Segmented cutover*. A segmented cutover occurs prior to the phaseout of the previous system (e.g., segment by region, by role, by function). Segmented cutover implies temporary coexistence of the replacement with the phased-out system.

  Typical reasons for segmenting a transition include:

  ▪ Need to handle a large number of transition requirements or readiness issues,

  ▪ Presence of complex transition requirements or issues,

- Need to make the transition at multiple sites,

- Urgency based on compliance issues, and

- Expediting the delivery of business value.

Prioritization schemes may be used as part of the preparation for a transition when it becomes necessary to conduct a transition in segments and to work on the segments with the highest priority.

o *Timeboxed coexistence.* A timeboxed coexistence of the replacement and the previous systems occurs with a final cutover on a specific future date. For this strategy, work conducted with the replacement follows the replacement's policies, procedures, and rules, while work conducted with the previous system continues to operate under its policies, procedures, and rules until the cutover date. This strategy is sometimes used for software projects involving architectural or database changes.

o *Permanent coexistence.* A permanent coexistence of the previous and replacement solutions exists as a permanent system (with all new business using the replacement solution).

Generally, massive cutovers present more business risk than cutovers that are segmented or timeboxed. Occasionally, however, that risk is acceptable.

Business analysis practitioners perform a cost-benefit analysis to determine which approach to use. They use risk assessments to identify and analyze the risks associated with each transition strategy. When analyzing each strategy to select the appropriate one, different perspectives are useful. Using critical thinking during facilitated workshops helps identify advantages and disadvantages for each approach. Other examples of questions or research that could be conducted to determine the most appropriate strategy are:

o What is the operational impact of having two solutions?

o Are there any customer-facing or marketing conditions that would require customers to interact with the new solution at the same time?

o Does the replacement solution involve software?

o Is it acceptable for some of the customer base to use the previous solution while others use the replacement solution?

- **Readiness assessment plan.** The business analysis practitioner develops a readiness assessment plan to determine the organization's ability and interest in transitioning to a future state using its new capabilities. This plan may take the form of a readiness checklist, where readiness characteristics can be checked off to reveal where there are transition elements still requiring attention.

The readiness assessment plan identifies the following items:

o What is to be measured for organizational readiness?

o How should organizational readiness be measured?

o What are the roles and responsibilities for assessing readiness?

The readiness assessment considers not only the organization's ability to make the change, but also its ability to use and sustain the solution and realize the value of the solution.

The assessment considers the cultural readiness of the stakeholders and the operational readiness to implement the change, the time frame between implementing the change and realizing the value, and the resources available to support the change effort. The business analysis practitioner uses the assessment to identify any gaps in readiness that are considered risks to achieving the end state and to develop risk responses for addressing them. At the end of the assessment, the business analysis practitioner generates a report that includes the results of the readiness assessment.

Case Study: Enable Organizational Transition

George and Rani collaborate to define transition requirements to address the transition from the current state of unpopular existing homes to the remodeled smart homes. They define transition requirements, including the following:

Transition Requirements

- During remodeling, homeowners will be housed in local accommodations arranged for by SCC for the duration of the work.

- Home appliances, furniture, and garage contents will be removed from the home during remodeling, as needed.

- Current homeowners will be trained on the IoT features in person while their homes are being remodeled.

- Two weeks of phone support for the IoT features will be available to homeowners after they move back into their homes.

Transition Plan

George develops a *transition plan* (see Table 5-1) and asks Rani to work with him because the transition includes the addition of the IoT features into the new home. Prior to planning, they remind each other that they are defining and designing the scope of the transition, but the actual transition work is the responsibility of the project manager. Together, they define the scope of the transition and the following high-level steps and activities.

Table 5-1. Transition Plan for Implementing IoT Features

Transition Plan												
Scope of transition: From the time that the home is ready to the time that the homeowner and family are moved back in and using the new features												
Activity	**Owner**	**Days**										
House Remodeling:		1	2	3	4	5	6	7	8	9	10	
Clear work area of construction materials.	Construction team	■	■	■	■	■	■	■				
Clean homes to be ready for homeowners.	Construction team					■	■	■				
Test public utilities.	Support team						■	■				
Confirm that residents are able to get through streets to their home.	Construction team								■			
Return appliances, furniture, and garage items—check functionality.	Construction team								■			
Remove materials and debris.	Construction team						■	■	■			
Prepare the home design.	Construction/ support teams	■	■	■	■	■						
Check the completion of the houses.	Support team										■	
Handle the checkout from accommodations.	Support team											
IoT-Based Smart Home:		1	2	3	4	5	6	7	8	9	10	
Run a successful pilot of IoT functionality.	Development team	■	■	■	■	■	■	■				
Prepare help desk to provide support for IT.	Support team	■	■	■								
Conduct required training for IoT to homeowners.	Support team								■	■	■	
Check the functionality of IoT features on devices.	Support team								■	■		

Transition Strategy

The home remodel implementation is done using a segmented approach. They modify five homes at a time and keep all construction consolidated to one block at a time to minimize traffic disruption. Getting the go/no-go decision is made for each segment of five homes. George and Rani develop a *readiness assessment checklist* to use to indicate that everything is okay to move ahead with implementation (see Figure 5-3).

(Continued)

Readiness Assessment Checklist

- ☐ Environmental safety (hazards removed)
- ☐ Public services are ready for use
  - ○ Electricity
  - ○ Water
  - ○ Wi-Fi
- ☐ Access
  - ○ Driveway and access to home are cleared
- ☐ IoT use
  - ○ Successful pilot of IoT functionality
  - ○ IoT help desk is ready to provide support
- ☐ Home
  - ○ Construction is completed
  - ○ Materials and debris have been removed
  - ○ Home is clean
  - ○ Appliances are in place and working
  - ○ Environmental settings are returned to normal
  - ○ Home design/construction support team is ready to provide support
- ☐ Homeowners
  - ○ Checked out of temporary accommodations
  - ○ Have been trained on how to use IoT and other new features

Figure 5-3. Readiness Assessment Checklist

Facilitate Go/No-Go Decision

The business analysis mindset requires a practitioner to work with key stakeholders and objectively review the results of transition activities and readiness assessments. This enables the decision makers to consider the organizational transition from multiple perspectives, the risks and issues for a go/no-go decision, and the courage to make the best decision in light of the business need.

Overview

In order to obtain a release decision, the business analysis practitioner needs to gather enough data and information to facilitate the decision for key stakeholders who are accountable for the solution (i.e., those who have a role to approve or sign off on the solution). This allows the key stakeholders to make the best decision for the business on whether to release the solution in whole, in part, or not at all.

The term *release* refers to the release of a solution or part of a solution into a production environment while the development team is still responsible for it. It may also refer to the release of a solution or a segment of a solution to the operational area that takes responsibility for it. Release either happens at the end of solution development or while developing the solution, depending on the selected development approach.

Business analysis practitioners provide stakeholders with sufficient and correct information to help them make the best decision for the organization to meet the business need and maximize and sustain the value of the solution as expressed in the business case. It is important to summarize evaluation results in a meaningful way because evaluations can produce voluminous amounts of information.

There are several pieces of information that need to be included, such as:

- Acceptability of the solution as evidenced by the evaluated acceptance results;
- Confirmation that the organization is ready for release;
- Confirmation that transition activities in preparation for release have been completed to the extent required, including coordination of this solution release with other concurrent releases;
- Acceptance of any remaining product risks and workarounds;
- Known issues and any workarounds that have arisen in response to those issues; and
- Communication conducted with the appropriate stakeholders based on the transition plan.

Depending on organizational norms, getting a release decision may include obtaining a sign-off. The formality of the sign-off depends upon the following:

- Type of project or program,
- Type of product,
- Project life cycle,
- Scale of the release, and
- Corporate and regulatory constraints.

Formal sign-offs for projects are a common protocol when one or more of the following characteristics are present:

- Projects with a line of business-wide or enterprise-wide impact;
- Products where errors or failure could result in death or an unacceptable level of risk to life, property, or financial solvency;
- Projects in organizations following strict predictive approaches; or
- Heavily regulated industries such as banking and insurance, medical devices, clinical research, or pharmaceutical companies.

Protocols for formal sign-off are agreed upon in planning and should include how it will be recorded, how it will be stored, and whether sign-off needs to be obtained when all of the signatories are physically together or whether it is acceptable to sign remotely.

Value of Facilitating Go/No-Go Decision

A go/no-go decision gives stakeholders who are accountable for the product the opportunity to decide whether to release the solution in whole, in part, or not at all. It creates an agreed-upon break between the development of a solution and the release of a solution for acceptance by the stakeholders.

This process helps gain stakeholder buy-in and mitigates the risk of resistance to the solution.

How to Facilitate Go/No-Go Decision

After gathering the necessary information and analyzing the results, the business analysis practitioner facilitates a meeting for a go/no-go decision on the solution (see Figure 5-4).

The following are some considerations when facilitating the go/no-go decision:

- Make go/no-go decisions as interactive as possible (in person, video communications, etc.) to encourage people to engage and ask questions so they understand the rationale for various perspectives.

- The stakeholders who were identified in the transition plan as having a role in approving or signing off on the solution are generally the individuals who make the go/no-go decision.

- Present the evaluation results in tabular or visual form to help decision makers grasp the impact and render a decision.

- Provide stakeholders with the opportunity to get answers to questions and debrief before the meeting.

- An agreed-upon decision model for how to reach a decision should already be in place.

- A "go" permits the release of the solution in whole or in part. A "no-go" either delays or disapproves the release of the solution.

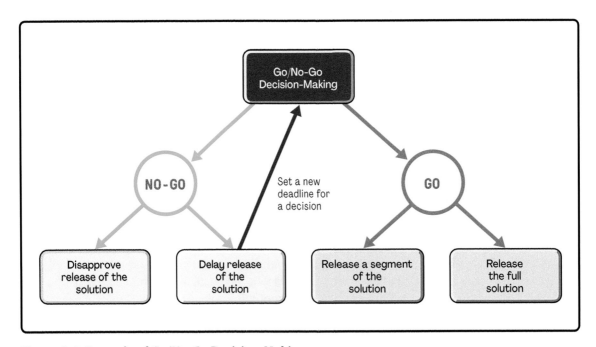

Figure 5-4. Example of Go/No-Go Decision-Making

Depending on organizational practices, a release decision may also involve obtaining a release sign-off. In an adaptive project approach, informal sign-off generally occurs at the end of each iteration. Formal sign-off, if required, occurs prior to any release of the solution to the production environment. In a predictive project approach, sign-off usually occurs at the end of the project, either immediately before or after release to production, or after the warranty period is complete.

Case Study: Facilitate Go/No-Go Decision

George presents the results of the readiness assessment, including the completed checklist, and refers to the decision-making process for moving ahead with the go/no-go decision as defined in the governance responsibility assignment matrix in the business analysis plan. Accordingly, Rani and George weigh in as consultants prior to the vote, and then the sponsor, project owner, project manager, construction lead, and sales and marketing lead all vote on whether to move ahead. Unanimity is required to move ahead. After George and Rani share their thoughts about the status of the transition, the others vote and agree to move ahead.

Evaluate Solution Performance

```
The business analysis mindset enables the business analysis practitioner
to objectively review the performance of the solution to determine if
it is meeting expectations and whether it needs to be refined, updated,
replaced, or discontinued.
```

Overview

Evaluate Solution Performance determines whether a solution or solution component that has been put into operation is delivering the desired business value. Business analysis work includes measuring the actual business value the solution is delivering against the business goals and objectives in the business case, and using the metrics identified in planning and potentially captured in a benefits measurement plan. Evaluation of solution performance typically occurs after a solution has been released. The business analysis practitioner performs this assessment during the development of a solution if an adaptive approach is used, or after the development of the solution is complete if a predictive approach is used. In both approaches, the evaluation of solution performance is performed at a higher level during portfolio or program activities rather than during solution development.

The evaluation of long-term or short-term performance is part of the evaluation of the business value realized by the implemented solution. Nearly all metrics considered in the evaluation of a solution are identified in the benefits management plan that is created during the development of the business case. These metrics can be evaluated periodically in the long term or short term to identify positive or negative performance trends.

The business analysis practitioner analyzes relevant business goals and objectives; evaluated acceptance results from a previous release; performance data; and baseline data, if available, to determine if value is being added and to identify reasons for better-than-expected results or causes for problems. Typical reasons for missed business value include:

- Technical causes,

- Business practices or constraints,

- Resistance to the product or the way it is intended to be used, and

- Opportunistic workarounds devised by those who use the product to get around real or perceived limitations of the solution.

The assessment of the performance of a product becomes an input into recommendations for improving the long-term performance of the solution and for portfolio and program management decisions about further enhancements to the product, decisions about new products, and decisions to replace or discontinue products.

Value of Evaluating Solution Performance

Evaluate Solution Performance provides tangible data to determine whether the solution in which the business has invested achieved, or is achieving, the expected business value and serves as the basis for decisions about future initiatives. The rationale for business value and the extent to which it has been achieved are important factors to consider when making product decisions within a portfolio or program.

The business analysis practitioner uses the evaluation to inform decision makers about whether to develop a new product or to enhance or retire an existing product. The outcome of this evaluation can lead the business analysis practitioner to find a problem or opportunity with the implemented solution.

How to Evaluate Solution Performance

Evaluate Solution Performance involves reviewing implemented or partially implemented solutions to assess whether the business value expected by the organization is being delivered (see Figure 5-5). If there is a significant variance between the expected and actual value, the business analysis practitioner analyzes the situation to uncover any problems or opportunities. If the business value exceeds the expected value, the analyzed situation is considered as an opportunity because the company can use it to further improve the positive results.

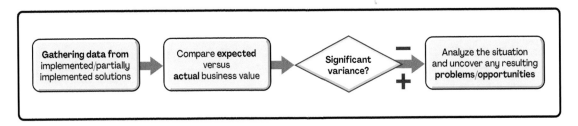

Figure 5-5. Evaluating Solution Performance

The assessment of business value is the result from comparing expected business value from a solution against the actual value that has been realized. If the desired business value was not achieved, the assessment includes an explanation for that.

Data to evaluate the business value are often measured by, and obtained from, the business area that takes ownership of the solution or by capability that has been built into the product. Business analysis techniques are used to analyze variations between desired and actual results as part of assessing the business value of the solution.

Any and all information captured as part of that solution can be analyzed to identify accomplishments and trends. For example, modern marketing organizations rely on analytics/ business intelligence capabilities to evaluate whether or not marketing campaigns achieved the desired changes in customer behavior in the long term.

Many measurements of business value need to take place after a solution is released and often need to be measured over the long term to detect trends. This requires an organizational commitment to invest in making the measurements and in building or purchasing the capabilities to measure business value when those capabilities would not otherwise be available. When such investments are not possible, organizations need to consider less costly, alternative ways to measure business value and possibly even consider whether the value of measuring the solution is worth it.

Case Study: Evaluate Solution Performance

George and Rani refer to the approved business case and benefits management plan to identify metrics they want to monitor to confirm that their solutions delivered the value expected in the business case. They also confirm that they have baseline metrics to compare with post-implementation metrics.

George identifies the Net Promoter Score® (NPS) obtained from the homeowners as the primary means of evaluating solution performance after the remodeling and IoT implementation. Rani identifies home sales as the primary means of evaluating solution performance. In addition, they intend to get subjective evidence of solution performance through interviews and focus groups. Table 5-2 provides some of the details of their *solution performance evaluation*.

Table 5-2. Solution Performance Evaluation Results

Solution Performance Metrics				
Metrics	**Baseline**	**Target Results**	**Time Frame**	**Owner**
Number of homes sold	25	125	By the end of the Q2 of the next year	Sales and marketing team
Net Promoter Score® (NPS)	-30	40	1 month after adjusting to the new home	Sales and marketing team
Metrics	**Baseline**	**1 month after completion of remodeling**	**3 months after completion of remodeling**	**6 months after completion of remodeling**
Expected number of homes sold	N/A	40	70	125
Actual number of homes sold	25	38	76	
Expected NPS	N/A	40	40	
Actual NPS	-30	20	22	

(Continued)

After 3 months, George and Rani review the results of their solution evaluation and are encouraged by the solution performance. They develop several strategies to enhance solution effectiveness.

To achieve the sales goal of 125 homes, they explore modifications to the marketing of the homes, including advertising mediums. Also, while they are impressed with the improvement in the NPS, there is a variation from the expected results, so Rani investigates the situation to identify problems or opportunities for improvement. She suspects changes to IoT support will contribute to better results and conducts research to confirm.

6

Business Analysis Stewardship Domain

Introduction

The Business Analysis Stewardship domain consists of activities performed and considerations pertinent to all business analysis work in order to increase the likelihood that business analysis work and results are effective, benefit the organization, and are supportive of the environment and community.

By doing stewardship work, the business analysis activities and solution effectiveness are tracked and measured regularly to make sure target benefits will be achieved, the business analysis capability and culture will be built and developed, and the potential ethical concerns will be considered consciously and seriously.

What to Expect in This Domain

This domain offers an approach to exercising good stewardship as the business analysis practitioner is conducting business analysis work.

Stewardship consists of three key practices that help the business analysis practitioner to (1) track and measure the effectiveness of business analysis work to make sure it provides the targeted value to the organization, (2) build up and enhance business analysis capability inside the organization or with stakeholders, and (3) consciously consider the impact to the community of business analysis work and solution applications. The three practices are:

- **Promote Business Analysis Effectiveness** enables practitioners to regularly track and check the effectiveness of business analysis work when performing business analysis activities, and after solution release to make sure business analysis work brings the organization business value as expected.

- **Enhance Business Analysis Capability** includes the activities involved in building up and promoting a business analysis culture in the organization by capitalizing on the opportunity to train, coach, and influence stakeholders to enhance the organization's capability to do good business analysis work.

- **Lead Business Analysis Work with Integrity** ensures that environmental, sustainability, social, cultural, and financial considerations are made when performing business analysis work, including the impact of business analysis activities, the proposed solution, and solution application after release.

Main Benefits of the Practices in This Domain

Stewardship refers to the principles underlying business analysis work and practicing with a business analysis mindset. For example, leading business analysis work with integrity builds up long-term trust and an open environment where stakeholders feel safe and comfortable, teamwork and collaboration are effective, and meaningful outputs are realized.

Only after the high-level stakeholders in the organization buy in to the value of business analysis work, will there be an opportunity to build a culture that champions business analysis practices from top to bottom throughout the organization. Meanwhile, business analysis practitioners can influence stakeholders who work together using formal or informal communications, training, and coaching, so they understand the value of business analysis work and enhance their capabilities to perform or support business analysis activities related to their daily work. These activities will help people understand and deal with business analysis work, which helps to make such work easier to perform and builds up a positive environment for business analysis practice.

Key Questions Answered in This Domain

- What is stewardship work when performing business analysis work?

- How is business analysis effectiveness promoted?

- How can a culture of championing business analysis practices be built in an organization and what are the benefits of such a culture?

- What are the benefits of leading with integrity for organizations, stakeholders, and business analysis practitioners?

Promote Business Analysis Effectiveness

The business analysis mindset embraces the spirit of continuous improvement and growth. It supports the business analysis practitioner in actively identifying opportunities to adapt processes and tools with the goal of delivering maximum value based on organizational needs.

Overview

Business analysis practitioners who actively examine business analysis activities and act on ways to promote improvement and maturation promote business analysis effectiveness. Promoting effectiveness is not a self-serving concept, where business analysis practitioners are looking to grow the practice in their organization by simply finding ways to add staff or other resources with no direct benefit to the organization. Rather, this growth concerns examining all aspects of the practice to identify and alleviate deviations or gaps in organizational expectations of knowledge, tools, processes, outputs, or outcomes.

Some organizations with mature business analysis processes and teams may already have well-established business analysis professional standards, performance measurements, and quality controls that directly guide the promotion of business analysis effectiveness. Other organizations or single proprietorships may have a more informal means of assessing success. The formality is not as important as the outcome: creating opportunities to improve business analysis performance.

Value of Promoting Business Analysis Effectiveness

Promoting business analysis effectiveness is the foundation of Business Analysis Stewardship. Without some means of assessing and reflecting on performance, business analysis practices can become stale, irrelevant, and decrease value delivery. It is even possible that business analysis practices could become roadblocks to success if the perceived risk of funding or participating in the activities is greater than the reward of the delivered value.

Business analysis effectiveness applies to all aspects of the practice, from assessing business value to evaluating the solution. It does not necessarily have to be complicated or time-consuming, depending on the nature of the practice. It is simply a way of thinking that underpins making the most of the available resources to reach future-state objectives. It can be as formal as establishing and measuring quarterly key performance indicators (KPIs) for an entire team of business analysis practitioners or as informal as a business analysis practitioner asking for feedback from a stakeholder during a coffee break. The value is in both proactively and retroactively identifying and acting on improvement opportunities.

How to Promote Business Analysis Effectiveness

The breadth and depth of the business analysis activities in an organization inform the business analysis practitioner about the extent of how business analysis effectiveness is promoted and carried out. There are many possibilities, depending on the available resources. Fundamentally, the business analysis practitioner needs to perform the following activities:

- Determine key areas of performance by examining which business analysis activities make the strongest contributions toward reaching the organization's goals. These activities could range anywhere from those related to stakeholder engagement, business analysis agility, or effectiveness of the overall solution after implementation. Work with the project team and other stakeholders when making these determinations as their voices are integral to business analysis success.

- Measure the key areas now to establish baselines, as well as over time to identify patterns in outcomes. Performance is measured in numerous ways, such as surveys, tracing, checklists, and other methods. Search for gaps to ensure that the processes and tools currently in use are adding value per practice and organizational expectations.

- Identify the causes for the gaps and act quickly to remedy them. These gaps represent precious improvement opportunities, which could include providing additional training for the business analysis practitioner, selecting more effective tools, implementing adaptive approaches, or reengineering processes to increase value and eliminate waste.

- Devote attention to quality to ensure that processes are being carried out and tools are being used consistently. Lack of consistency can cause confusion or dissatisfaction within the project team and among the stakeholders.

With attention to promoting business analysis effectiveness, the business analysis practitioner can create a regular cadence in supercharging the business analysis practices to boost planning and execution, better engage stakeholders, and over time, grow the organization to become more proactive and value-driven.

Case Study: Promote Business Analysis Effectiveness

George and Rani both approach the business analysis work they do with a commitment toward stewardship of their activities as well as the outputs and outcomes of their business analysis activities. They both strive to improve the effectiveness of business analysis work within their organization by assessing how anyone doing business analysis work is performing, and they look for opportunities to improve business analysis performance and outcomes. George and Rani both promote business analysis effectiveness with their commitment to continuous improvement and are open to ideas from others about how to do business analysis work more efficiently or increase the value of business analysis work. While they both seek to maximize the value of business analysis work and grow the maturity of business analysis practices within their organization, the ways they do so are different.

George's effort to grow the business analysis practice at SCC includes measuring the outcomes of business analysis work. He captures metrics to identify potential problems and opportunities for improvement of business analysis activities. During planning on the house remodeling project, George identifies metrics to monitor as indicators of how well he and the team are performing, and he captures them in a matrix to track them through the end of organizational transition and solution evaluation (see Table 6-1).

Table 6-1. Business Analysis Performance Metrics

Metric	How Measured	Month 1	Month 2	Month 3	Month 4
Quality of business analysis deliverables	Percentage of business analysis practitioner's time spent answering questions about documents and deliverables	21	18	11	
Stakeholder satisfaction with the value of the business analysis work being done	Average of responses to one-question survey using a 1 (low) to 5 (high) rating scale	3.75	4	4	
Team's ability to effectively collaborate	Facilitated team self-assessment (Needs improvement, Good, Very good, Excellent)	N	G	V	

Rani's ability to promote business analysis effectiveness is addressed through the iterative process itself. Two events enable Rani and the team to improve the business analysis work they are doing and help grow the maturity and effectiveness of the team's business analysis work.

First, the iteration review with the customer provides feedback on how well the team elicited the customer's needs, how well those needs were communicated to the team developing the solution, how well the approach to prioritization is working, and other key business analysis activities and outcomes that are part of each iteration.

Second, the team's retrospective following the review provides the team with an opportunity to evaluate how well they performed throughout the iteration. Considering that much of the work they do in each iteration is fundamentally business analysis, such as defining user stories, defining acceptance criteria, prioritizing stories, facilitating a shared understanding of the "requirements," ensuring that solution requirements and other details are in scope and add value, etc., Rani feels confident that she and the team are strong stewards of their business analysis work and that the process itself ensures that they continuously improve.

Enhance Business Analysis Capability

A business analysis mindset enables the business analysis practitioner to help others tap into their business analysis capabilities to promote the business analysis mindset throughout the organization. Practitioners using a business analysis mindset create a safe environment for cultivating a healthy business analysis culture by reserving judgment, being inclusive, and being flexible.

Overview

Business analysis practitioners enhance business analysis capabilities within the organization and among practitioners of all types when they help others recognize their own business analysis work and inspire them to use their business analysis skills. When people do not recognize their work as business analysis work, there is a tremendous opportunity for improving the outcome of their efforts, whatever they may be.

An effective business analysis practitioner helps to build a business analysis culture inside the organization, where people learn to recognize what they are doing as business analysis work. Whether through training at a lunch-and-learn session, cocreating process models to understand how a particular business function works, or investigating new models, the business analysis practitioner can spark curiosity to expand business analysis capability throughout the organization. Business analysis practitioners, as stewards of business analysis, promote learning and collaboration among practitioners of all types to support the growth of business analysis capabilities. Business analysis practitioners also help develop the confidence in others to experiment and apply the business analysis practices they know.

Value of Enhancing Business Analysis Capability

As the business analysis practitioner enhances business analysis capability throughout the organization, the language, practices, and tools of business analysis become more familiar. Individuals become more comfortable doing their own business analysis work as they are able, and they are savvier about when to call in more experienced business analysis practitioners. This helps mitigate the stress resulting from constrained business analysis resources, such as a single business analysis practitioner supporting multiple projects.

Enhancing business analysis capability is key to accelerating business analysis effectiveness and promoting organizational agility. As the business analysis practitioner evangelizes business analysis, the value of business analysis is more readily recognized and the organization supports business analysis practices more enthusiastically. Through stewardship activities around enhancing business analysis capability, the ability of people to do the work and collaborate with others to derive the benefit of good business analysis practices grows, and people feel empowered and are enabled to do business analysis work. Individuals are more likely to be proactive to receive benefits sooner rather than waiting for a "business analysis practitioner" to get them started. Overall, the organization develops a healthier, more responsive business analysis culture and reaps the benefits of business analysis work when and where it is needed.

How to Enhance Business Analysis Capability

Business analysis practitioners are in a position to enhance business analysis capability every time they interact with stakeholders, whether they are team members, business people, or others in the organization, by being transparent and recognizing teaching moments in those interactions. Using a business analysis mindset, business analysis practitioners open themselves and others up to learning through patience and a focus on shared understanding.

For example, when collaborating with stakeholders in elicitation workshops, model storming with team members, or reviewing development results at the end of an iteration, the business analysis practitioner enhances capability in simple ways such as:

- Telling the stakeholders what tools are being used,

- Inviting participants to experiment with leading the session, or

- Facilitating exploratory discussions about other applications for the tools being used.

Fundamentally, business analysis practitioners enhance business analysis capability when they make business analysis easy to understand and use. Business analysis practitioners remove barriers to benefiting from business analysis when they invite stakeholders to worry less about whether their use of a practice or tool is "right" and focus more on learning through collaboration. They make business analysis accessible to stakeholders when they identify when someone is doing business analysis work, even if they don't recognize it as such.

Enhance Business Analysis Capability is done by exercising one's passion for the discipline of business analysis with a business analysis mindset and sharing that passion with others.

Case Study: Enhance Business Analysis Capability

George and Rani strive to enhance business analysis capability throughout the organization. When working with stakeholders, George makes a concerted effort to explain his tools and techniques in simple language to prompt questions. He frequently creates time in his team meeting agendas for just-in-time learning sessions and asks a team member to share a challenge they are facing or how they have used a particular technique. Rani's team has high expectations for learning from one another, and learning is very much a part of their team culture.

George and Rani both cocreate whenever possible and have experimented with hosting very short, online, informal facilitated discussions with business analysis practitioners and other stakeholders to share business analysis tools and techniques. These sessions are no more than 15–20 minutes long and are an effective way to communicate the value of what they do and encourage stakeholders to develop their own business analysis skills. Last week's session on how to use a definition of done (DoD) to set expectations regarding any work effort was well received.

Lead Business Analysis Work with Integrity

Using a business analysis mindset is the bedrock of leading business analysis work with integrity. Thinking holistically and comprehensively enables business analysis practitioners to understand far-reaching implications of solutions and business analysis work. A healthy skepticism enables practitioners to ask questions where others may be complacent. This mindset guides business analysis practitioners to creatively explore ways to meet the business need while acting as stewards of the environment, sustainability, communities, and organizational financial well-being.

Overview

To lead business analysis work with integrity is to be transparent about the commitment to business analysis values, such as ethical, environmental, sustainability, social, cultural, and financial considerations, and to promote the transparency of that commitment in an organization's business analysis work.

Solutions to business problems continue to challenge ethical boundaries. Solutions involving artificial intelligence (AI), machine learning (ML), questions of privacy, and data security are examples that put the business analysis practitioner squarely in the middle of complex ethical questions. The incentive to capitalize on new technologies is compelling. The concerns about new technologies are daunting. The business analysis practitioner who leads business analysis work with integrity surfaces these concerns and has the courage to ask questions about whether there is potential harm to the natural or human environment. As the custodian of the solution, the business analysis practitioner is in a strategic position to engage others in those discussions as the details of the solution emerge.

To lead business analysis work with integrity means that as a business analysis practitioner conducts their work and collaborates with others, they are acting as stewards in the following ways:

- **Environmental steward.** The business analysis practitioner is open and honest about the impact a solution will have on the physical and natural environment. If a solution is harmful to the environment, they will not recommend it and will inform others about the issue.

- **Sustainability steward.** The business analysis practitioner advocates for solutions that conserve resource consumption, reuse resources when possible, and utilize Earth-friendly resources whenever possible. In addition, they ensure transparency about solution options regarding sustainability.

- **Social and cultural steward.** The business analysis practitioner seeks to fully understand the impact solutions may have on people, cultures, and communities. The business analysis practitioner assesses the positive and negative impacts of a solution, ensures they are understood by the stakeholders, and collaborates to find ways to mitigate those negative risks.

- **Financial steward.** The business analysis practitioner avoids conflicts between their personal financial interests and those of their organization or clients, and they contribute to the short- and long-term value of organizational assets through a commitment to ethical and prudent financial decision-making regarding product and solution life cycles.

Value of Leading Business Analysis Work with Integrity

Leading business analysis with integrity inspires trust and confidence in business analysis and the work of the business analysis practitioner. Leading boldly and transparently promotes awareness of biases and opens the business analysis practitioner and others to a variety of opinions. As solutions are being considered, defined, refined, and implemented, stakeholders are more confident that ethical concerns about the solution, including environmental, sustainability, social, cultural, and financial considerations, will have been discussed.

Business analysis practitioners who lead business analysis work with integrity contribute to psychological safety in their organizations, more meaningful and inclusive collaboration, and overall business analysis maturity.

How to Lead Business Analysis Work with Integrity

A business analysis practitioner who leads business analysis work with integrity asks questions as they collaborate with others to conduct business analysis activities and generate outputs and outcomes. Questions include:

- Is this activity, output, or outcome being done or created in such a way as to be environmentally friendly?

- Does this activity, output, or outcome minimize the consumption of resources and maximize the use of reused or recycled resources?

- Does this activity, output, or outcome have a supportive, helpful, or neutral impact to the social or cultural fabric of people and their communities?

- Is this activity, output, or outcome financially free of conflicts of interest and does it make good financial sense for the organization in the long and short term?

The business analysis practitioner asks these questions openly to stakeholders in meetings, interviews, workshops, and any context in which those who can contribute to the answer are present. If the answer to any of these questions is "no," the business analysis practitioner leads business analysis work with integrity by engaging stakeholders to explore options, and they engage decision makers to discuss those options.

Case Study: Lead Business Analysis Work with Integrity

Leading business analysis work with integrity is embedded in everything George and Rani do as business analysis practitioners. Their stewardship in this regard manifests in several ways:

- When sourcing materials for both projects, George and Rani confirm that the materials being used are consistent with the company's commitment to environmental sustainability and support the goal of being a global leader in the green home industry. When vendors provide materials that are not consistent with the goals that are being considered, George and Rani are quick to point it out to the project manager and those making purchasing decisions.

- A couple of key reasons behind the business problem are related to homes not being culturally suited to how most families in the area use the spaces in their homes. George and Rani arrange for a cultural anthropologist to give a talk about the local culture, which gives the architecture and construction teams insight into how to modify the homes to be more appealing to the area residents. Surveys done after implementing the changes reveal that these were the most impactful changes in generating enthusiasm for the homes and ultimately generating sales.

- Rani lived for a short time near the community where the remodeling and IoT projects are being implemented, so she is familiar with some of the names of businesses and individuals in the area. Further, she is good friends with the owner of one business that is being considered for a technology contract on the IoT initiative. Rani makes sure her supervisor, project manager, and the procurement authority for that contract are aware of her connection to that business.

7

Models, Methods, and Artifacts

This section provides a generic definition for most of the tools and techniques that support the practices covered in Sections 2 through 6 referenced in the case study. These tools and techniques appear in a separate section because they are universal and may be used repeatedly throughout a project, program, or portfolio. One of the most powerful aspects of these tools and techniques is that the output of one may be the input to another. The tools are referenced in the practices to provide context for the application of the tool, but that does not restrict the tool to that practice or the practice to that tool.

PMIstandards+™, an online library of PMI content, can be a useful reference for researching these tools and other tool options. PMI members can access PMIstandards+ at https://standardsplus.pmi.org/.

Overview

This section defines guidelines on utilizing tools to support the practices presented in this practice guide. The instructions are represented via infographics that help business analysis practitioners quickly consume and apply the information. Each infographic answers three questions to assist in the quick consumption, as described below.

- **What?** This is a high-level description of the tool or technique. This should answer the question: "What is this tool or technique?" This may also include a statement about context that addresses "when."

- **So What?** This section includes the reason for using the tool or technique. It answers the question "why" you would use it and outlines the purpose and value of the tool.

- **Now What?** This section describes how to use the tool or technique, including numbered steps when applicable. A visual model or picture is included, when possible.

List of Tools and Techniques

The tools and techniques appear in alphabetical order as follows:

- Acceptance criteria
- Affinity diagram
- Brainwriting
- Business rules
- Buy-a-feature
- Capability table
- Feasibility analysis
- Five whys
- Focus group
- Force field analysis
- Key performance indicators (KPIs)
- MoSCoW
- Onion diagram
- Persona
- Product tree
- Readiness assessment
- Real options
- Requirements traceability matrix
- Stakeholder engagement assessment matrix
- Story mapping
- Survey
- Survey data analysis
- Wireframe

ACCEPTANCE CRITERIA

What?

Acceptance criteria are a set of conditions that are defined and must be met before deliverables or features captured in user stories are accepted. Acceptance criteria are typically written for each deliverable and/or user story and determine whether the feature described meets the user requirement. It is a form of requirements documentation. Typically, they are written before the development team begins working on the deliverable so that the team understands exactly what is required for an item or feature to be satisfactorily completed and can write tasks associated with creating that item or feature.

So What?

Typically, acceptance criteria are used to determine if the deliverable or feature can be "accepted" as developed. Acceptance criteria are used by the testing team to verify that a feature or deliverable is functioning as intended. Writing the acceptance criteria in a manner that walks the testing team through the feature helps ensure that it is ready for a production environment and can eliminate future issues.

Now What?

Before work can begin on a deliverable or user story, the business analysis practitioner should ensure that at least one acceptance criterion is written. If a deliverable has more than three, it might be good for the team to consider dividing the deliverable or user story into two or more to help the team to implement the feature as quickly and efficiently as possible. The acceptance criteria must be independently testable and should focus on the final product or increment. Development team members work together with the product owner and business analysis practitioner to write the acceptance criteria. The criteria should be written in easy-to-understand language, avoiding technical jargon. Anyone on the team should be able to look at the acceptance criteria and know exactly what is needed for the deliverable or feature to be considered satisfactory when delivered.

A concept that is sometimes confused with acceptance criteria is the definition of done (DoD). The DoD identifies the criteria that must be met for all aspects of the solution increment, including completion of all corporate documentation, regression testing, security validation, and production support readiness. That is, the DoD applies to the entire product increment, whereas acceptance criteria are specific to a deliverable, user story, or feature.

Deliverable: Submit Form

Acceptance Criteria

☐ When the save button is clicked, the form lights up red if a required item is missing.

☐ After the form submission, a notification tells the user whether the form submission was successful or there was an error.

Figure 7-1. Acceptance Criteria

AFFINITY DIAGRAM

What?

Affinity diagrams are the result of affinity mapping, which is a method for organizing or classifying ideas into groups. The mapping process helps teams arrange raw, unfiltered ideas into categories that are discovered through the process of clustering.

This process can be used when a team needs to order and collate their individual thoughts about a subject. The act of clustering becomes a single-group activity in which the participants collectively discover themes, similarities, and differences among their independently offered ideas.

So What?

The affinity diagram and affinity mapping exercise make it possible for a group to generate responses or actions when it is difficult to know what to do because of the apparent disconnection of unrelated ideas. It is typically used after a brainstorming session in which contributors have generated a large number of ideas and it is difficult to see how they may be related. Without affinity diagramming after a brainstorming session, the team is unable to see patterns or themes that can enable them to develop constructive responses to the problem or idea for which the brainstorming was done. Affinity diagramming illuminates how ideas are related and enables the team to respond strategically to the myriad ideas offered.

Now What?

An affinity exercise tends to be more effective when it is conducted by a team of subject matter experts and led by a facilitator who is familiar with the subject. Each step shown below may be done in various ways. For example, the ideas that provide the inputs to the affinity diagram (Step 2: Generate ideas) may be created through any type of brainstorming or idea-generation exercise. Many tools exist for doing affinity diagramming virtually.

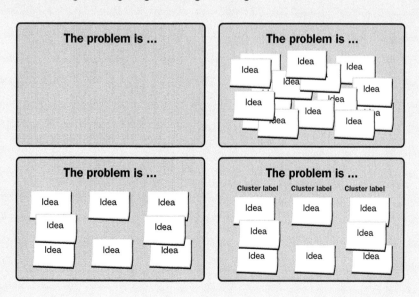

continued

Figure 7-2. Affinity Diagram

AFFINITY DIAGRAM *continued*

1. Present topic
Present the topic to the group. For example, it may be a problem to solve or an issue that needs clarity. Post the topic for the group to see.

2. Generate ideas
Decide whether participants will work individually, in small groups, or all together. Invite participants to generate ideas in response to the topic. For example, they may come up with potential solutions to the problem or aspects of the issue to be considered. The rules of brainstorming will apply in this step, i.e., this is the time for idea generation, not idea evaluation.

3. Collect ideas
Collect all ideas generated, one at a time. Confirm that all ideas are clearly understood by everyone. Each idea should be placed on the board randomly; where the ideas are placed in this step does not matter.

4. Group ideas
Participants begin moving ideas on the board and grouping them into clusters of similar ideas or ideas that have some affinity with other ideas. Ideas may get moved from cluster to cluster as participants share their different perspectives. This step may be done without talking to promote equal participation from everyone.

5. Label clusters
Once the movement of ideas has stopped and all ideas are settled into clusters, the group chooses a label for each cluster. Once labeled, the group can more easily see how to respond to problems or categories that will help understand a situation.

Figure 7-2. Affinity Diagram (continued)

BRAINWRITING

What?

Brainwriting is an approach to brainstorming or sharing ideas and thoughts in a group setting. Rather than typical brainstorming in which participants share their ideas verbally, brainwriting involves participants contributing their ideas by first writing them down individually. Individually generated ideas are then collected and shared anonymously.

So What?

Traditional brainstorming is a great way to generate many ideas in a short period of time. However, the ideas of people who are uncomfortable sharing their ideas verbally in a group are often missed, while those who aren't afraid to state their ideas out loud end up dominating the discussion. By giving all participants time to individually write down their ideas and then share them anonymously, everyone's contributions are considered, generating a wider breadth of ideas and better results.

Now What?

Many approaches to brainwriting may be used. Often, the first part of brainwriting is done in silence, so that the idea generation portion of the session is done without talking. Stages of the session may be timeboxed to keep the sessions focused. Steps in a brainwriting session typically include the following:

1. A problem or objective is stated and posted for everyone to see.

2. Each participant generates their ideas in response to the stated problem or objective.

3. When finished or time is up, participants pass their ideas to someone else who then adds to the ideas.

4. Ideas are passed around to everyone, so all participants can make their contributions to all ideas generated.

5. After all ideas have made the rounds, all ideas are shared.

Figure 7-3. Brainwriting

BUSINESS RULES

Business rules describe policies, standards, or regulations that constrain how the business operates. They describe the decisions a business has made about how they want to operate. Examples include how something is calculated, how discounts are applied, the sequence in which something is done, or limits. The business rules may apply to an initiative, department, or even entire organization, and they must be observable, written in business language, and have consequences if not followed. They are system-agnostic and define how the business operates regardless of systems and technology.

So What?

Identifying business rules is critical to business analysis because solution requirements need to support the business rules. For example, consider this business rule: *All bank employees receive a .025% discount on loan rates.* If this is the case, then solution requirements must be defined to enforce that rule. While all organizations have business rules, they are often undocumented. The business analysis practitioner needs to maintain visibility of the business rules when eliciting requirements to ensure that the requirements support the business rules that dictate how the business operates.

Now What?

Business rules may be captured and referenced in a variety of ways. For example, a business rules catalog may be created if not already available. They may be referenced in a requirements traceability matrix (RTM) to illustrate how they are supported with requirements. In adaptive environments, business rules may be posted on the product backlog or somewhere visible and included in the elaboration of user stories.

Recipe Box				
BR ID	**Business Rule Title**	**Business Rule Description**	**Type (fact, computation, constraint, other)**	**References**
BR01	Recipe email opt-in	Recipe emails will only be sent to customers who have opted in and have a valid email address.	Constraint	See corporate email policy
BR02	No PII in recipe email	Recipe emails will not contain any personally identifiable information (PII).	Constraint	See corporate email policy
BR03	Ingredients in stock	A new recipe will not be sent when more than 10% of the stores have a restocking status of greater than 24 hours for any of the ingredients.	Computation	Will use inventory reporting system

Figure 7-4. Business Rules

BUY-A-FEATURE

"Buy-a-feature" is a simple and effective collaborative game for helping people choose the features they would like to be available for a given product. The buy-a-feature game works by giving participants a limited amount of imaginary cash, naming the price for each feature, and asking them which features they would buy with the money they receive.

So What?

The buy-a-feature prioritization approach can help a product team that is struggling with a complicated feature "wish list" and limited development resources. Buy-a-feature activities can help put these limited resources into perspective for stakeholders who seem to want everything all at once.

Now What?

There are several ways to structure and facilitate the buy-a-feature collaborative game. Below are the basic steps for facilitating this game:

1. **Prepare the set of features you need to prioritize:** List all the critical features that need to be prioritized with stakeholders.

2. **Set a price for those features:** In this step, two different approaches can be taken.

   A – Determine the price for each feature based on the actual cost of development, time, and resources. Negotiation is highly recommended to gain valuable insights.

   B – If it is difficult to set a price, let participants split the money they receive across features, however desired. Priority is determined by which features receive the most money.

3. **Give participants a budget and send them shopping:** Once the group of participants has been selected and the items on the list have been explained, give each participant a fixed amount of play money and send them shopping.

4. **Observe and learn as the participants discuss, negotiate, and buy:** This is the stage where the product team can gain valuable insights into the group's priorities and needs. Their discussions and efforts to collaborate will provide important clues about what aspects of the product are considered most important and why.

5. **Review the participants' purchases and have them explain their decisions:** When participants have spent all their play money, it's time to discuss their decisions as a group.

Figure 7-5. Buy-a-Feature

CAPABILITY TABLE

What?

Capability tables are used for analyzing capabilities in a current or future state. The model can provide an easy way to visualize current problems, the associated root causes, and the proposed new capabilities or features that will address the problem or opportunity.

So What?

The technique can be applied to depict the relationships among a situation, its root causes, and the current capabilities, alongside the features or capabilities required to address the problem or opportunity and achieve the future state. This technique is a good choice for a model to relate the information obtained during the current state analysis with the information resulting from future state discussions.

A capability table is a useful tool to map the results of the root cause analysis, which could be represented in a fishbone diagram. Thus, it is applicable after the root cause analysis. Mapping allows all stakeholders to see the big picture and guide the discussion to identify associated current or required capabilities or features.

Capability tables can provide different perspectives when defining the solution components, which helps ensure that each component addresses the root cause of the problem or opportunity.

Now What?

The following figure shows an example of how a capability table might be structured.

Problem/Current Limitations	Root Cause(s)	Current Capability	New/Future/Required Capability	Component/Deliverables to Fill the Gaps
Problem	1st root cause	· Current capability · Current capability	· New capability · New capability	· New deliverable · New deliverable
	2nd root cause	· Current capability · Current capability	· New capability · New capability	· New deliverable · New deliverable
	3rd root cause	· Current capability	· New capability	· New deliverable

Figure 7-6. Capability Table

FEASIBILITY ANALYSIS

What?

Feasibility analysis is an in-depth analysis of proposed solutions from different perspectives that is based on several factors to help ensure the proposed solution options are viable and can be successfully implemented.

So What?

Feasibility analysis is an important step in business analysis and can help avoid costly mistakes and ensure the long-term success of the solution. This is an initial risk assessment that is a preliminary study to determine the feasibility of a proposed solution and to help decision makers decide whether or not to proceed with the solution.

Now What?

Organizations may dictate that the results of the feasibility analysis be captured in a formal document using an approved template, but the level of formality followed depends on organizational standards.

Common elements for consideration in feasibility analysis include the following:

- **Constraints.** Any limitations that restrict the option under consideration.
- **Assumptions.** Any factors that are unknown and are assumed to be true, real, or certain for each option without actual proof or demonstration.
- **Product risks.** Uncertain events or conditions that may have a positive or negative effect on the successful delivery of the solution.
- **Dependencies.** Any relationships upon which a solution depends for successful implementation.
- **Culture.** An enterprise environmental factor that can impact both the success of the business analysis effort and the solution implementation.
- **Operational feasibility.** The extent to which a proposed solution meets operational needs and requirements related to a specific situation. It also includes factors such as sustainability, maintainability, supportability, and reliability.
- **Technology feasibility.** An analysis to determine the extent to which a technology exists in an organization to support a potential solution and, if not present, how feasible it would be to acquire and operate the needed technology.
- **Time feasibility.** An analysis to determine how well a proposed solution can be delivered to meet the organization's needed time frame.
- **Cost-effectiveness feasibility.** The high-level economic feasibility of a potential portfolio component, program, or project, taking into account both financial benefits and costs.
- **Value.** The business value that the solution option will provide to the organization. It includes a discussion of how value may change over time.
- **Validation.** An assurance that the solution will meet the needs of the customer and other identified stakeholders. Each option will require a different approach and level of effort to validate its alignment with the business objectives.

Figure 7-7. Feasibility Analysis

FIVE WHYS

Five whys is a method of identifying the possible root causes of a problem or event by iteratively asking "why." It is part of the tools and techniques of the Lean Six Sigma approach, and is remarkable in its simplicity.

Although it is called "five whys," it is not required to ask "why" exactly five times. There might be fewer or more "whys" being asked. The five is more a representation of the depth of the root cause than the number of times asked.

Most of the time, a problem has many root causes. Keeping track of them might become difficult and even tedious. If the problem's root cause is complex, the group might forget what is a root cause of what. Therefore, the five whys technique is often used in combination with the fishbone (Ishikawa) diagram.

So What?

Business analysis practitioners may use five whys in interviews or team settings to identify root causes or for clarifying business problems to ensure the right problem is being solved before exploring solutions. It can help show the path from root cause to effects. When used with a fishbone diagram, it can also serve to illustrate the network of root causes currently being investigated.

Now What?

Keep in mind:

- The approach is limited to the team members' knowledge.
- A common challenge is to keep the group from focusing on symptoms rather than real root causes.
- It has been noted that results are not repeatable because different teams will find different root causes for the same problem.
- If not used with a fishbone diagram, there is a tendency to arbitrarily isolate a single root cause.

Key elements:

- Write a problem statement with the group and make sure everybody agrees on it.
- Use sticky notes, paper, or a (virtual) whiteboard to write down questions and root causes to keep the process flowing.
- Don't jump to conclusions (don't skip a level). When someone suggests a root cause to a "why" question, make sure the suggestion is really the immediate cause. Remember that there can be many causes.
- A good way to help make sure that something is a cause is to run the problem backward:
  - The maintenance was not done; therefore, the belt was not changed at the end of its life.
  - The belt was not changed at the end of its life; therefore, the belt was too old.
  - The belt was too old; therefore, it broke ... and so on.
- Make sure to rely on facts and knowledge, not guesswork.

continued

Figure 7-8. Five Whys

- Assess the problem, not the people. That is another way of saying do not focus on the symptoms of a problem, i.e., what makes it apparent.
- Remember that human error, inattention, and similar elements are not root causes.
- Be careful about how the question "why" is asked. Use different questions to understand "why" without asking why, because it can cause people to become defensive.

Example:

Problem

The Jefferson Memorial in Washington, D.C., USA, was wearing out much more often than it should and needed frequent repainting due to repeated pressure washing of the monument. This upkeep was very costly and impacted the visitor experience.

Solution

Five whys helped identify the root cause of the problem and an effective solution: Turn the lights on after dusk when the bugs are not active. By delaying the lighting of the monument a short time, the bugs stopped swarming it, birds left far fewer droppings, and the paint did not deteriorate from too-frequent washings. By determining the root cause and solving it, the team saved countless future dollars in labor, paint, and energy by not repainting as frequently, and more visitors were able to enjoy the monument when it was not being cleaned or painted.

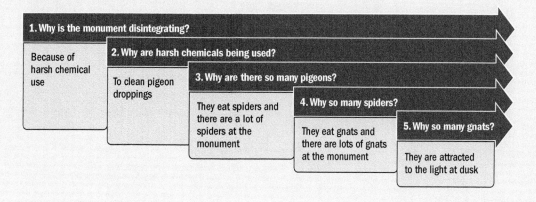

Figure 7-8. Five Whys (continued)

FOCUS GROUP

What?

A focus group is a qualitative research method in which a small group of individuals is brought together to discuss and provide feedback on a particular product, service, or topic. The group is typically led by a facilitator who asks open-ended questions and encourages discussion among the participants. The goal of a focus group is to gather detailed insights and opinions from a diverse set of perspectives, which can then be used to inform decision-making or further research.

So What?

Focus groups provide an opportunity to elicit stakeholder knowledge or assess design options for a product. The objective of this activity is to capture participant expectations and attitudes about a proposed solution, service, or result. Sessions are facilitated in a manner that allows for healthy team dynamics, a free flow of ideas, and a sufficient level of unbiased feedback.

The outputs of successful focus groups should be considered as important factors when making product decisions. The wide variety of members in a focus group provides objective input from participants who have varying levels of proximity to the product objective.

Now What?

The focus groups will provide several different types of feedback on which to base future analysis. The table below represents several ways the feedback can be utilized. Part of the analysis is to understand the feedback points and determine how that feedback can be utilized.

Feedback Utilization	Definition
Understanding customer needs	The main purpose of a focus group is to gather insights about customer needs, preferences, and behaviors. A business analysis practitioner can use this information to gain a deeper understanding of the customer and identify potential opportunities for improving products, services, or customer experience.
Identifying trends	A business analysis practitioner can use the output of a focus group to identify patterns and trends in customer feedback. This can help the business to prioritize areas for improvement and allocate resources more effectively.
Validating hypotheses	Focus group feedback can be used to validate hypotheses or assumptions that the business has about its customers or market. For example, if the business is considering launching a new product, the focus group can provide feedback on whether the product meets customer needs or if there are any potential roadblocks.
Refining strategies	Focus group feedback can help a business analysis practitioner to refine existing business strategies or develop new ones. By understanding customer needs and preferences, the business can adapt its strategies to better align with customer expectations and improve overall business performance.

Figure 7-9. Focus Group

FORCE FIELD ANALYSIS

What?

Force field analysis is a tool used to identify and analyze the forces that may impact a decision, change, or project. It is based on the idea that any change or decision is influenced by both driving forces, which support and encourage the change, and restraining forces, which resist or oppose it.

To conduct a force field analysis, a business analysis practitioner first identifies the specific change or decision that is being considered. Next, the practitioner lists the driving forces and restraining forces that may impact that change or decision. These forces can be internal to the organization, such as policies, processes, or resources, or external, such as market conditions, competitors, or regulatory requirements.

So What?

Once the driving and restraining forces have been identified, the business analysis practitioner can analyze their relative strengths and determine whether the driving forces are strong enough to overcome the restraining forces. The practitioner can also identify strategies or actions that may be able to increase the strength of the driving forces or reduce the strength of the restraining forces.

Force field analysis is a useful tool for understanding the factors that may impact a change or decision, and for developing strategies for addressing or overcoming any challenges or obstacles. It can be used in a variety of contexts, including project management, business planning, and organizational change.

Now What?

Steps to initiate a force field analysis:

1. **Identify the problem or change initiative.** This could be a business process, product, or goal to be achieved.

2. **Assemble the appropriate team members.** Include stakeholders who are involved in or affected by the problem or change initiative. The team should include individuals who have a range of perspectives and expertise.

3. **Define the current situation.** Gather information on the current situation, including the driving forces and restraining forces that are affecting the problem or change initiative. This can be done through surveys, interviews, and data analysis.

4. **Evaluate the strength or weight of each force based on its impact on the problem or change initiative.** The overall driving forces can be compared against the overall restraining forces to determine the net acceptance for the change. This will help determine where to focus efforts to achieve the desired outcome.

5. **Develop an action plan.** Based on the weights of the driving and restraining forces, develop an action plan to address the restraining forces and strengthen the driving forces. The action plan should include specific steps, time lines, and responsibilities for each team member.

By following these steps, a business analysis practitioner can initiate a force field analysis to gain a better understanding of the problem or change initiative, identify the driving and restraining forces, and develop an action plan to achieve the desired outcome.

continued

Figure 7-10. Force Field Analysis

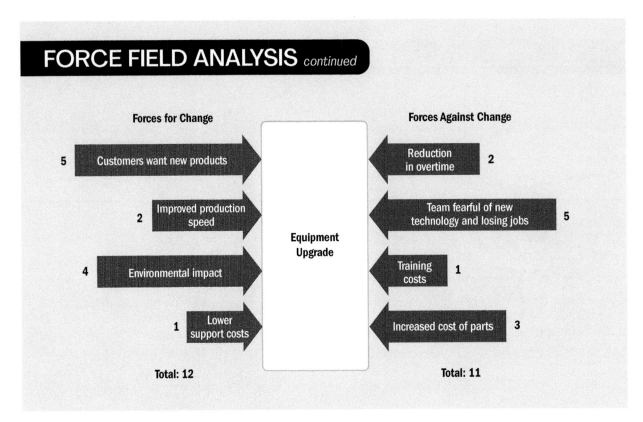

FORCE FIELD ANALYSIS *continued*

Forces for Change

Forces Against Change

5 Customers want new products

Reduction in overtime 2

2 Improved production speed

Team fearful of new technology and losing jobs 5

4 Environmental impact

Training costs 1

1 Lower support costs

Increased cost of parts 3

Equipment Upgrade

Total: 12

Total: 11

Figure 7-10. Force Field Analysis (continued)

KEY PERFORMANCE INDICATORS (KPIS)

What?

Metrics are a set of measurements or quantitative indicators used to track and evaluate the performance of a system, process, or activity. Metrics are essential for business analysis as they allow organizations to measure and evaluate the performance of various business processes and activities. Not all metrics are key performance indicators (KPIs), but a metric becomes a KPI when it is selected as a key indicator of performance that is critical to achieving specific business objectives and is used to measure progress toward those objectives. By tracking KPIs, organizations can stay focused on their objectives and make data-driven decisions that lead to improved results and increased success.

So What?

Business analysis practitioners will often focus on KPIs to identify the specific areas where the organization's performance is not meeting expectations to develop a targeted plan to close those gaps. This allows the organization to prioritize its efforts and resources toward the most critical areas and ensure it is making progress toward the overall objectives. KPIs are also used to evaluate the effectiveness of a solution.

Now What?

In short, KPIs provide a clear and measurable way to assess performance and identify areas for improvement, which is essential when conducting a gap analysis and developing a plan to close performance gaps or evaluate solution effectiveness.

The organization must decide which of the available metrics are the most important and which most accurately reflect performance. Tips for identifying KPIs include:

KPIs Should Be	KPIs Should Not Be
Tied to a component of the business value stream	Arbitrary things that are measured "because we can"
Specific measures that provide insight into important aspects of business performance	Complex measures subject to various interpretations
Objective measurements of the performance of a business process	Goals or objectives (although they link requirements and solutions to organizational goals and objectives)
Able to be compared to previous results so progress can be demonstrated	Frequently changed so the business cannot track progress
Useful for stakeholder and interdepartmental collaboration	Difficult for other teams to understand
Focused on what is most important for measuring business performance	Vague or overwhelming collections of measurements that have varying degrees of measuring performance

Examples of KPIs:

- **ROI** — Return on Investment
- **YOY** — Year Over Year Growth
- **AOV** — Average Order Value
- **CAR** — Cart Abandonment Rate
- **NPS** — Net Promoter Score®

Figure 7-11. Key Performance Indicators (KPIs)

MoSCoW

What?

MoSCoW is a prioritization technique that is an initialism for "must have," "should have," "could have," and "won't have." Business analysis practitioners may use MoSCoW to prioritize requirements, features, and functions, and to select the most valuable options so that appropriate resources are made available to develop and achieve the goals. MoSCoW can be used in predictive, hybrid, and adaptive project environments.

So What?

MoSCoW can be used by business analysis practitioners in various situations when interacting with stakeholders, such as meetings, interviews, focus groups, and other formal or informal settings. Some prioritization techniques don't always engage participants in enough discussion to make good decisions. For example, when prioritizing using high-medium-low, many options end up categorized as "high" even if they are not really high priorities. MoSCoW is a good way for business analysis practitioners to facilitate an open, more substantive discussion and reach a consensus.

Now What?

While MoSCoW is a common technique, teams should begin prioritization using MoSCoW with an agreed-upon understanding of what it means. The M, S, C, and W typically mean the following:

Must have: The requirement or feature must be achieved completely, or the business target will not be met and the product will not be acceptable. Anything categorized as a "must have" is critical to success and resources need to be available to ensure it is delivered.

Should have: "Should have" items are important to the business target or final product. However, if the item cannot be achieved, the solution or product may not be perfect, but will still be okay and acceptable. The team can consider completing it if resources are still available after the "must have" items are completed.

Could have: These items are less important features, and if they are not included, the impact will be limited. They are considered the "nice to haves." The team may complete these after the delivery of the "must haves" and "should haves."

Won't have: Anything categorized as a "won't have" will not be included. Even if it is important, it may still be labeled as "won't have" due to resource or cost issues. Defining "won't have" features is important so the team understands whether that means "won't have" at any point or "won't have" at this time. That clarification helps team members focus on the previous three types.

continued

Figure 7-12. MoSCoW

MoSCoW *continued*

Must Have	Should Have
• No shortcut • Nonnegotiable • Solution is not viable without it	• Essential but not vital • Workaround needed in case it is missing • Solution is still viable without it
Could Have • Desirable • Optional features • Nice to have	**Won't Have** • Irrelevant features • No real impact • Out of budget • At this time or not at all

Figure 7-12. MoSCoW (continued)

ONION DIAGRAM

What?

An onion diagram can be a powerful tool for conducting stakeholder analysis in any initiative. It is named as such because, like the multilayered vegetable, it is a visual representation of the multiple layers of engagement involved with an initiative.

So What?

By analyzing stakeholders using an onion diagram, business analysis practitioners can identify stakeholders at various levels and develop strategies to engage and communicate with them effectively. This can help ensure a project is aligned with stakeholder needs and expectations and can improve the likelihood of success.

Now What?

An onion diagram is typically arranged into four layers to visually represent the stakeholder relationship to the initiative. Optionally, an additional core layer can be added for identification of the initiative if needed.

Layer 1: Team that is executing the project or creating the product (i.e., project team members).

Layer 2: Teams or individuals who are directly impacted by the change that will occur with the new initiative or product. An example is a team that will be using a new solution being introduced to the business.

Layer 3: Teams or individuals who regularly interact with those in Layer 2. This layer could include the executive sponsor or other departments that may experience secondhand impacts from the change.

Layer 4: Any external stakeholders who can directly influence requirements or will be impacted by the changes brought about by the initiative or product. Examples are government agencies, regulators, customers, or suppliers.

The best way to build the diagram for an initiative is to identify the layers starting from the center. The innermost layer represents the team members working on the initiative. As the business analysis practitioner works through each layer, they should carefully consider who may be impacted and how.

After creating the initial draft, the practitioner should validate the information prior to proceeding with stakeholder engagement and requirements planning.

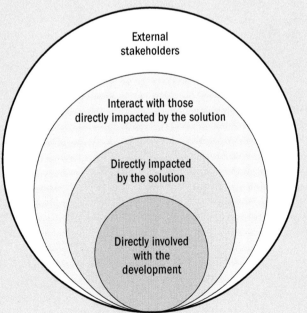

Figure 7-13. Onion Diagram

PERSONA

A persona is a fictional character that represents a particular user profile or stakeholder segment. It is an archetypical user of a solution and illustrates a type of person who would interact with it, including their goals, behaviors, motivations, environment, demographics, and skills. Personas are used to generate empathy by giving the team "someone" to relate to, instead of just thinking and talking about generic "users." This technique helps generate empathy by creating perspective, emotional connection, and real-world examples.

So What?

Personas contribute to a better understanding of customers, which can inform solution development, product design, and marketing decisions. Business analysis practitioners can use personas in several ways to inform and guide solution development:

1. Prioritizing features,
2. User-centered design,
3. Testing and validation,
4. Customer empathy, and
5. Cross-functional collaboration.

By incorporating empathy into the persona development process, teams can create personas that are accurate, relatable, and truly represent the needs and perspectives of the customer. Understanding and empathizing with these personas can help the team make better decisions about how to meet their needs, resulting in a better product and an improved customer experience. Personas facilitate understanding of the customer in order to delight them.

Now What?

Personas will be as unique as the user profiles they represent, and every team will create them in a way that reflects what distinguishes that user from other profiles, what the team thinks is important about the archetype, and what will best help the team "relate" to the user profile. This graphic is an example of a persona for a customer profile that purchases the luxury model of a product.

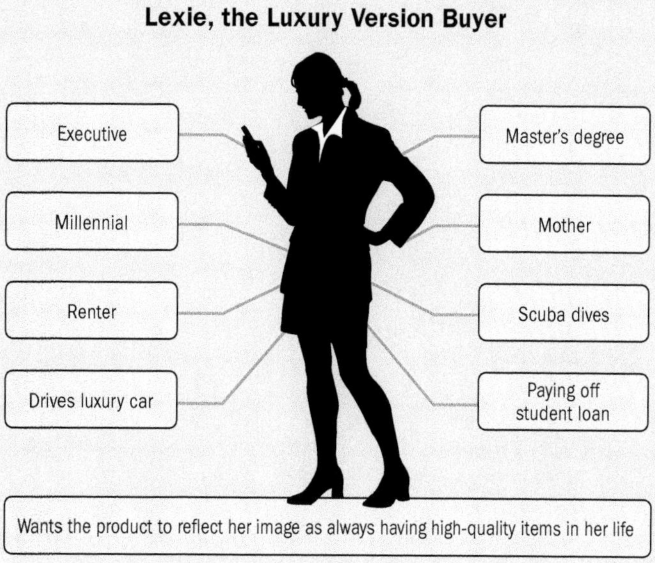

Lexie, the Luxury Version Buyer

Executive
Millennial
Renter
Drives luxury car

Master's degree
Mother
Scuba dives
Paying off student loan

Wants the product to reflect her image as always having high-quality items in her life

Figure 7-14. Persona

PRODUCT TREE

What?

The product tree is a visual tool that helps stakeholders envision the primary functions of a product (the branches) sitting on the base (trunk) of the requirements. The roots and trunk of the product tree represent the technical requirements, or infrastructure, that is needed to hold up the branches and leaves. The branches of the tree are the primary functions of the product being built. The leaves represent future enhancements or new features. Additional items that could be added to the product tree include apples and seeds. The apples could symbolize a return on investment, and the seeds on the ground surrounding the tree may represent deprioritized items.

So What?

A product tree is used during brainstorming activities and workshops with stakeholders to help the team envision the growth of the product and any proposed features. It helps the team prioritize feature requests, manage stakeholder input, and showcase previously unknown requirements. A product tree is a fun, collaborative way to organize and prioritize the many requests and ideas that customers and other stakeholders present to the team.

Now What?

Each team member has the opportunity to add features to the product tree. When done in a group setting, each member can use sticky notes to place items on the product tree. Features that are related can be clustered or grouped around a branch or subbranch. As the group discusses each feature, they can move them along the tree, helping to prioritize the different features. The highest priority items should be placed near the bottom of the tree and closer to the trunk. Anything farther out will be worked on later or may ultimately be "pruned" from the tree if it is determined it is no longer a priority. Some questions that can be asked while pruning and prioritizing the tree include:

- Are any branches too heavy or lacking features?

- Do any features require more research?

- Are the roots (infrastructure) strong enough to hold the branches (features)?

- Are there any requirements missing that would help support the branches?

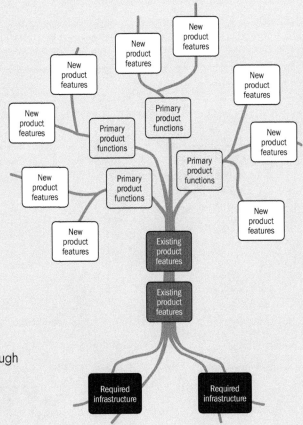

Figure 7-15. Product Tree

READINESS ASSESSMENT

A readiness assessment is conducted to assess an organization's readiness to transition the solution to maintenance and operations (M&O) and/or the production environment. The assessment facilitates a comprehensive analysis of all facets of readiness.

So What?

Readiness assessments determine the ability and interest of an organization to transition to the future state or use its capabilities. The assessment is used to identify any gaps in readiness that are considered risks to achieving the end state, along with risk responses for addressing them.

The business analysis practitioner may conduct multiple readiness assessments to ensure that the organization is adequately prepared. These iterative readiness assessments confirm that the organization, team, process, system, and product are prepared for the transition and operation of the solution.

Now What?

A readiness assessment may take the form of a report that provides the results of a readiness evaluation, or it may take the form of a readiness checklist, where readiness characteristics can be checked off to reveal where transition elements still require attention. There are often unique aspects to each transition that stem from the specific products or organization being evaluated for readiness. There are also some generic aspects to transition readiness assessments that apply to all organizations or all organizations within an industry. A few examples may include:

- **People readiness.** Are people ready to use the new solution? Have they been trained? Will they be able to interact with the solution as needed?

- **Data readiness.** Has data been validated internally or by any necessary third parties?

- **Production environment readiness.** Has the necessary hardware and/or software been installed, and is it ready to support the solution? Has appropriate testing been done? Have technical security concerns been addressed satisfactorily?

- **Transition and production support readiness.** Are operations and support services ready to answer questions and provide support? Are release notes and workarounds that may be needed documented? Are continuity and contingency plans and procedures in place?

- **Cultural readiness.** Is the organizational culture supportive of the change so that people are open-minded and ready to work through challenges and obstacles? Are champions engaged and helping stakeholders see the benefits?

Figure 7-16. Readiness Assessment

REAL OPTIONS

What?

Real options is a decision-making thought process for dealing with uncertainty and risk. It is a simple and powerful approach that helps anyone make more informed decisions by understanding and responding to the psychological effects of uncertainty regarding their behavior, both as individuals and in organizations. Real options is a technique that allows teams to determine when to make decisions, not how or why. Real options thinking means:

- A decision does not need to be made immediately; however, the decision maker is aware of a deadline for making the decision.
- The decision maker keeps as many viable options open for as long as possible.
- The decision maker actively gathers information to maximize their understanding of each option until the moment a decision must be made.
- Decision makers only commit when they must or when they have a good reason to.

So What?

Later in the decision-making process, decision makers know more and have more information, which allows them to better deal with uncertainty.

Decision makers are also better able to deal with risk when they defer decision-making; they can wait and see what happens. If there are several options open, they can go with the one that best deals with the risk when it arises.

Now What?

Follow these steps to practice decision-making with real options:

1. For each decision, identify the available options.
2. Identify the last point at which a decision can be made, i.e., the conditions to be met in order to make a commitment (decision time means the deadline for option implementation). The first decision is made before the first option expires.
3. Until this expiration date, the decision maker can continue to search for new options and refine or extend the existing options.
4. Identify more option(s) for each condition case and identify, in advance, which option to exercise under a given condition.
5. Attempt to delay the timing of the decision. Often, this is free or very low cost. To do this, decision makers should be able to implement the option as quickly as possible. Work on ways to speed up the downtime.
6. Understand that cost optimization is different from revenue optimization or risk mitigation. Sometimes it pays to invest in more than one option, even though it may cost a little more. Afterall, options have value.
7. Wait to make decisions ... and wait ... and wait ... until the conditions are met.
8. When decision makers must make a commitment and act, they should do so as soon as possible. They can then proceed with confidence, knowing they have made the best possible decision.

continued

Figure 7-17. Real Options

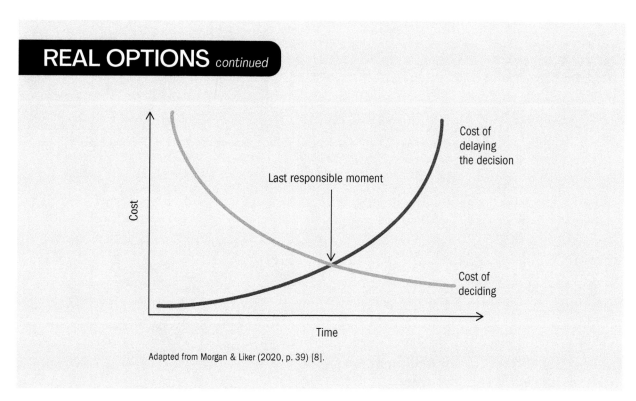

Adapted from Morgan & Liker (2020, p. 39) [8].

Figure 7-17. Real Options (continued)

REQUIREMENTS TRACEABILITY MATRIX

What?

A requirements traceability matrix (RTM)—also called a traceability matrix or coverage matrix—is a grid that identifies the bidirectional links between solution requirements and the business and stakeholder requirements from which they are derived, and the deliverables that satisfy the solution requirements, as well as links to other solution requirements. It contains a short description of each requirement and the facts or attributes about it that define its key information. It may also include deliverables, artifacts, business rules, models, and other elements of solution information related to a requirement. An RTM is typically used in a predictive environment, although a lighter version is sometimes used in adaptive environments. In some organizations, the RTM becomes the main requirements document.

So What?

An RTM helps ensure that each solution requirement adds value and is in scope by linking or tracing it to the business need, business goals and objectives, and project goals and objectives. Tracing solution requirements to stakeholder requirements helps ensure that the solution requirements meet the stakeholder expectations. Other reasons to use an RTM include:

- Lessens the likelihood of missing requirements;
- Helps ensure that approved requirements are delivered at the end of the initiative;
- Helps manage changes to requirements by illustrating dependencies among requirements;
- Provides visibility into the impacts of changes to requirements and supporting deliverables; and
- May be an asset in release planning when it includes the product development stage or project phase.

Now What?

A business analysis tool or any kind of spreadsheet application may be used to create an RTM. Creating links to documents and other elements in the matrix can enhance the utility of even a simple spreadsheet. Whether to use an RTM and what information to be traced is decided in planning based on the type of project, the needs of the team and the stakeholders, the degree of details to which business analysis planning is being done, governance that may impose tracing requirements, and other planning considerations. The benefits of tracing need to be weighed against the cost of the time it takes to create, maintain, and use the RTM. The business analysis practitioner should only include the requirements attributes (characteristics) and elements that will provide value to the team and any stakeholders who may be consuming the information in the RTM. Examples of attributes often found in RTMs include:

- Requirements ID (a unique identifier that does not change)
- Brief description
- Objectives
  - o Business goal/objectives
  - o Project goal/objectives

continued

Figure 7-18. Requirements Traceability Matrix

- Product development stage or project phase
- Work breakdown structure (WBS) (a cross-reference to deliverables as identified in the WBS)
- Status (e.g., active, approved, deferred, canceled, added)
- Rationale for inclusion (why the requirement is important to include)
- Priority (how important it is)
- Owner (who will own it once implemented)
- Source (where the requirement came from)
- Author (who wrote the requirement)
- Version
- Date completed
- Stability (how likely it is to change)
- Complexity
- Acceptance criteria

Requirements Traceability Matrix									
Project Name	**ABC OMS**								
Cost Center	**Operations–Customer Care**								
Project Description	**Development of ABC Order Management System**								
Business Requirement Description	Stakeholder Requirements	Functional Requirement	Functional Requirement Description	Objectives BO = Bus Obj PO = Pro Obj	Test Case (TC) ID	Business Rule	Priority MoSCoW	Status AC = active AP = approved DE = deferred CA = canceled AD = added	Source
BR001 – Change Order System	SR03	FR03.001	Update inventory	BO1, BO4 PO1, PO2	TC.011 TC.012	Inventory must be updated at the time of the order (B.Rule 20)	M	AP	Logistics manager – interview 03/16/20XX
		FR03.002	Change location	BO2, PO2	TC.014	–	M	AD	Logistics manager – interview 03/25/20XX
	SR05	FR05.008	Display cost change	BO2 PO1	TC.023 TC.024	–	S	AC	Accounting manager – interview 02/22/20XX
BR002 – Change Customer System	SR10	FR10.021	Add multiple missing addresses	BO5 PO2	TC.39	Customers may have up to four mailing addresses (B.Rule 44)	C	DE	Sales team – workshop 03/02/20XX

Figure 7-18. Requirements Traceability Matrix (continued)

STAKEHOLDER ENGAGEMENT ASSESSMENT MATRIX

What?

When planning stakeholder engagement, business analysis practitioners can use a stakeholder engagement assessment matrix to compare current engagement against the desired engagement level.

So What?

The stakeholder engagement assessment matrix can help assess what level of engagement is needed from different stakeholders at different stages of the business analysis activities. Once the stakeholders are mapped in the matrix, the business analysis practitioner can determine where there are gaps and decide on the steps to take to address those gaps.

Now What?

The stakeholder engagement assessment matrix uses the following classifications for each stakeholder:

- Unaware
- Resistant
- Neutral
- Supportive
- Leading

The current state is identified with a "C," and the desired state is identified with a "D." An additional column may be added to show a stakeholder's power and interest.

A business analysis practitioner uses certain parameters to determine the stakeholders' levels of engagement, such as their needs, interests, and influence on the area under assessment.

The stakeholder engagement assessment matrix should be used throughout the business analysis activities. As engagement changes, the business analysis practitioner can move their current state on the matrix to the appropriate column. If gaps change, and especially if the gap becomes larger, practitioners should reevaluate what may be leading to the gaps and whether they are effectively communicating with stakeholders.

Stakeholder	Unaware	Resistant	Neutral	Supportive	Leading
Stakeholder 1		C		D	
Stakeholder 2	C		D		
Stakeholder 3				CD	
Stakeholder 4					CD
Stakeholder 5			C		D
Stakeholder 6			C	D	

Figure 7-19. Stakeholder Engagement Assessment Matrix

STORY MAPPING

What?

Story mapping (also called user story mapping) is a method developed by Jeff Patton that provides a "big picture" context for the product backlog. The "map" provides an additional dimension to the backlog by arranging user activities along a horizontal axis in the general order in which the user would perform them. Lower-level tasks and stories derived from those activities are then ordered from top to bottom along the vertical axis according to priority and criticality for the user to reach their goal.

So What?

Story maps paint a complete picture of how a product will be used, which is often lost in a "flat" product backlog that may include a large number of user stories. They are also a means of discovering user stories by starting with what the user does and then breaking down those activities into lower-level tasks and, ultimately, user stories.

Story mapping helps avoid the risks of incremental delivery that can happen with a typical two-dimensional product backlog. For example, a collection of user stories may be ordered at the top of the backlog, but releasing them as increments may fail because their value is only realized when implemented with stories of lower priority on the backlog. That is, the stories at the top of the backlog may be the top priority, but it may not make sense to release them as a set, given how users use the product.

Now What?

The components of a story map include:

- **User role:** A story map tells a story about a type of user doing something to reach a goal. They are identified at the top of the map.

- **The backbone:** Activities and tasks at a higher goal level make up the backbone of the map and are arranged in a narrative flow. These are similar to epics—big stories with lots of steps.

- **Narrative flow:** The left-to-right axis is time. Arrange activities and tasks from left to right in the order of telling a story about how the user would perform the activities.

- **User tasks:** These are decomposed activities on the backbone represented as short verb phrases. User tasks are the basic building blocks of the map. User tasks make great story titles and creating a map can help practitioners to discover stories. These can include subtasks, alternative tasks, exceptions, or other details.

- **Delivery/release slice:** The smallest number of tasks (and related user stories) that allow users to reach their goal is the minimum functionality in each release, typically referred to as the minimum viable product (MVP). Additional slices identify groups of tasks that may be included in subsequent releases.

continued

Figure 7-20. Story Mapping

The terms used for the layers of a story map vary. Many practitioners identify three layers on story maps as follows:

- **The backbone:** The backbone is the top row of a story map. It outlines the essential capabilities the system needs to have. The backbone typically includes high-level features or epics.

- **The walking skeleton:** The walking skeleton is immediately below the backbone. When the epics in the backbone are decomposed, the stories in the skeleton emerge—these are the stories that make the product minimally functional, and hence, are often collectively referred to as the minimum viable product (MVP). The walking skeleton is the full set of end-to-end functionality that the user requires for the solution to be accepted or considered functional.

- **User stories:** Below the walking skeleton, there are additional stories, which are ordered top to bottom along the vertical axis. These stories are aligned with the epics in the backbone and will provide the user with the lower-priority functionality they will need in future releases.

After identifying the layers in the story map, releases can be identified as horizontal lines, dividing and grouping functionality based on priority and the capacity of the development team.

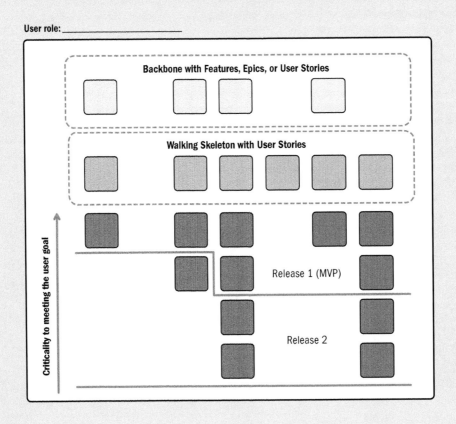

Figure 7-20. Story Mapping (continued)

What?

A survey is a method of collecting information using sets of questions designed to quickly accumulate information from a large number of respondents, with the goal of understanding populations as a whole. Respondents represent a diverse population and are often dispersed over a wide geographical area. Surveys provide an important source of data and insight.

So What?

The survey is beneficial for collecting a large amount of information from a large group over a short period of time at a relatively small cost. When confidentiality is made part of the process, participants may be more willing to provide information in a survey that they would not otherwise provide in a face-to-face forum like an interview.

Now What?

There are four modes of surveys that are commonly used:

- Face-to-face surveys,
- Telephone surveys,
- Self-administered paper and pencil surveys, and
- Self-administered computer surveys (typically online).

Consider the following recommendations when creating a survey:

- **Define the objective.** There is no point to conducting the survey if the objective and outcome are unplanned before deploying it.
- **The number of questions.** The number of questions used in a market research study depends on the end objective of the study. It is important to avoid redundant questions in any way possible.
- **Simple language.** One factor that can lead to a high dropout rate in surveys is if the language is difficult for respondents to understand.
- **Question types.** There are several types of questions that can be included in a survey. It is important to use the question types that provide the most benefit to the research while being the easiest for respondents to understand and answer. The formulation of the questions is often closed-ended, but usually some open-ended questions can be used.
  - Closed-ended questions. These questions offer a limited choice of answers, including "yes/no." Limited-choice questions are easier to quantify and analyze.
  - Open-ended questions. Respondents can answer in any way or to any extent they wish.

Open-ended responses can provide more substance than closed-ended questions but are more difficult and time-consuming to analyze.

- **Consistent scales.** If using questions with rating scales, make sure the scales are consistent throughout the study.
- **Survey logic.** Logic is one of the most important aspects of survey design. If the logic is flawed, respondents will not be able to proceed or take the desired path.

Figure 7-21. Survey

SURVEY DATA ANALYSIS

What?

Survey data analysis is the process of turning the raw material from survey data into insights and answers that can be used to improve things for the business. It's an essential part of doing survey-based research.

So What?

Often, analyzing data from surveys is an underestimated skill. Interpreting what consumers are trying to communicate can inform the organization's marketing strategies, messaging, and new products or services, possibly for years to come. So, it is crucial to get it right.

Getting it wrong could have disastrous effects on the business. The organization could launch the wrong product, publish an offensive ad, or target the wrong potential customers, all because surveys were analyzed unsuccessfully.

Now What?

The specific steps to take when analyzing a survey include:

- Look at the results of the survey as a whole.
- Determine the demographics of the respondents.
- Compare responses to different questions to identify discrepancies.
- Find connections between specific data points with layered data.
- Compare new data with previous data.
- Always be critical.

Top mistakes to avoid include:

- Being too quick to interpret survey results,
- Treating correlation like causation, and
- Missing the nuances in qualitative natural language data.

Figure 7-22. Survey Data Analysis

WIREFRAME

What?

In business analysis, wireframes are used to ensure that the project team and business stakeholders are aligned with the requirements when initially planning out the system to be designed. A wireframe is a low-fidelity drawing of the proposed application that shows the key elements of the user interface with the intended layout. The wireframe also shows how the system should work by walking through the different screens of the application.

So What?

When designing a wireframe, the key is to keep it simple. It should not take very long for a business analysis practitioner to design the wireframe diagrams. The wireframe should represent all of the key requirements and details; however, it does not need to be fancy. For example, if an image needs to be added to the application, a box can be added that indicates an image will go there, without needing to add the actual image.

Now What?

As the business analysis practitioner gathers requirements and begins to understand what the application may look like, they can begin sketching the details out in sample wireframes. These wireframes will be used in discussions with the business stakeholders and project team to ensure everyone is on the same page. During the discussions, stakeholders may ask for the design to be a little different or may notice that a requirement is missing. The development team will also be able to discuss if the requirements are attainable or if there are other pieces that need to be added to meet the expectations of the business stakeholders.

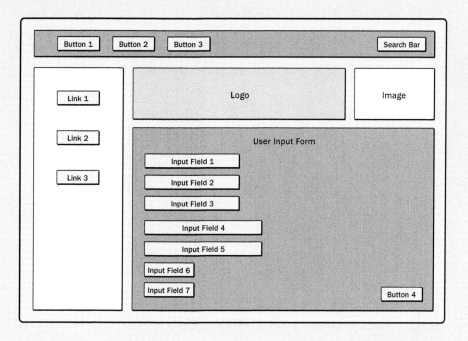

Figure 7-23. Wireframe

Additional Resources

In addition to the tools and techniques referenced in this practice guide, further guidance on business analysis activities can be found in PMIstandards+®, a dynamic platform that is a companion to PMI content. Use the QR code below to find more related subject matter. PMI membership or a subscription is required.

References

[1] Project Management Institute. (2017). *The PMI guide to business analysis*. Author.

[2] Project Management Institute. (2017, September). *Business analysis: Leading organizations to better outcomes*. Author. https://www.pmi.org/business-solutions/white-papers/business-analysis-leading-organizations-to-better-outcomes

[3] Taylor, P. (2023, May 2). *Digital transformation – statistics & facts*. Statista. https://www.statista.com/topics/6778/digital-transformation/#topicOverview

[4] BrainStation. (2023). *Are business analysts in high demand?* BrainStation. https://brainstation.io/career-guides/are-business-analysts-in-high-demand

[5] Coate, P. (2021, January 25). *Remote work before, during, and after the pandemic*. NCCI. https://www.ncci.com/SecureDocuments/QEB/QEB_Q4_2020_RemoteWork.html

[6] Upwork. (2020, December 15). *Upwork study finds 22% of American workforce will be remote by 2025*. [Press release]. https://www.upwork.com/press/releases/upwork-study-finds-22-of-american-workforce-will-be-remote-by-2025

[7] Straker, K., & Nusem, E. (2019, March). Designing value propositions: An exploration and extension of Sinek's "Golden Circle" model. *Journal of Design, Business & Society*, *5*(1), 59. https://doi.org/10.1386/dbs.5.1.59_1

[8] Morgan, P., & Liker, K. (2006). *The Toyota production development system: Integrating people, process, and technology*. Productivity Press.

Appendix X1
Contributors and Reviewers of *Business Analysis for Practitioners: A Practice Guide*

The Project Management Institute is grateful to all of the contributors for their support and acknowledges their outstanding contributions to the project management profession.

X1.1 Contributors and Reviewers

The following contributors and reviewers had input into shaping the content of this practice guide. Individuals listed in bold served on the *Business Analysis for Practitioners: A Practice Guide* – Second Edition development team. Inclusion of an individual's name in this list does not represent their approval or endorsement of the final content in all its parts.

Andrea Brockmeier, PMI-ACP, PMI-PBA, PMP, Development Co-Lead

David Davis, PMI-PBA, PMP, PgMP, Development Co-Lead

Rouzbeh Kotobzadeh, PMI-PBA, PMP, PfMP, Lead Content Developer

Kaisheng (Charles) Duan, DBA, PMI-PBA, PfMP

Amy Bretherick Gangl, MBA, CBAP, PMP

Louis-Charles Gauthier

Michelle Johnston, CAPM, PMP

Kerreen Andrea Wilson

Michael Adegbenro, PE, PMP

Michael Agbodzah, MC-AM, PMI-ACP, PMP

Nahlah Alyamani, PMI-ACP, PMP, PgMP

Hossein Ansari, PMI-PBA, PMP

Kenichiro Aratake, PMP

Ma. Loricar Arboleda

Sharaf Attas, PMI-RMP, PMP

Leonel I. P. Augusto

Casey Ayers, MBA, CBAP, PMP

Aleksander Binder

Ellie Braham, ATP, RIMS-CRMP, PMP

Andrew W. Burns Sr.

David Claassen, MAIPM, CPPP

Charlene L. Cornwell, CBAP, PMI-ACP, PMP

Pronob Das

Murat Dengiz

Nedal Dudin, PMI-ACP, PMI-PBA, PMP

Gobi Durairaj, PMI-ACP, PMI-PBA, PMP

Amir Kamali Far, MSPM, PSM I, PMP

Jean-Luc Favrot, PMI-ACP, DASSM, PMP

Donna Fok, CISSP, PMP

Sheethal Francis, PMP

Pamela Goodhue

Lydia Goodner, PMP

Weibin Gu, PMI-ACP, PMI-RMP, PMP

Edward Hung, PMI-ACP, PMI-PBA, PMP

Syed Aafaq Hussain, PMI-PBA, PMP

Tony Jacob, CM-Lean, PMI-PBA, PMP

Rami Kaibni, CBAP, PgMP, PfMP

Rachel Keen, PMP

Henry Kondo, PMP, PgMP, PfMP

Aboozar Kordi

Cheryl Lee, CBAP, PMI-PBA, PMP

Lydia Liberio, MBA, PMP

Ramiro A. Sánchez López, PhD, PMP

Mahdi Moein, PMI-PBA, PMP, PfMP

Subrat Kumar Mishra

Iman Mohammadi

Syed Ahsan Mustaqeem, PE, PMP

Asaya Nakasone, PMP

Laura Lazzerini Neuwirth, AHPP, AgilePgM, PMP

Spencer Oklobdzija, PMP

B K Subramanya Prasad, CSM, PMP

Zulfiqar Ali Qaimkhani

Hossein Rahmatjou

P. Ravikumar, PMP, PgMP, PfMP

Arsalan Rejalizadeh

P. Seshan, PMI-ACP, PMI-RMP, PMP

Chihiro Shimizu

Farshad Shirazi

Sam Stevenson, MPH, PMP

Tetsuya Tani, CBAP, PMP

Laurent Thomas, PMI-ACP, DASSM, PMP

Esteban Tissera

Qayamuddin Usmani

Ebenezer Uy, PMI-ACP, PMP

Hany Zahran

X1.2 PMI Staff

Special mention is due to the following employees of PMI:

Kristin Hodgson, CAE, CSPO

Leah Huf

Christie McDevitt, APR

Kim Shinners

Glossary

Acceptance Criteria. A set of conditions that are met before deliverables are accepted. In business analysis, acceptance criteria are built to evaluate the product requirements and solution. See also *deliverable* and *requirement*.

Adaptive Life Cycle. A project life cycle that is iterative and incremental.

Affinity Diagram. A group creativity technique that allows large numbers of ideas to be classified into groups for review and analysis.

Assumption. A factor that is considered to be true, real, or certain, without proof or demonstration.

Benchmarking. The comparison of actual or planned practices, such as processes or operations, to those of comparable organizations to identify best practices, generate ideas for improvement, and provide a basis for measuring performance.

Benefits Realization Plan. A document outlining the activities necessary for achieving the planned benefits. It identifies a time line and the tools and resources necessary to ensure the benefits are fully realized over time.

Brainstorming. In business analysis, brainstorming is an elicitation technique that is performed in a group setting and led by a facilitator to engage stakeholders to quickly identify a list of ideas for a specific topic in a relatively short time period.

Business Analysis. The set of activities performed to support delivery of solutions that align to business objectives and provide continuous value to the organization.

Business Analysis Practitioner. Any individual doing the work of business analysis, regardless of title.

Business Case. A documented economic feasibility study used to establish validity of the benefits to be delivered by a portfolio component, program, or project.

Business Need. The impetus for a change in an organization, based on an existing problem or opportunity. The business need provides the rationale for initiating a program or project.

Business Objective. Measurable representation of the goals the business is seeking to achieve. Business objectives are specific and should align to the organizational objectives.

Business Rule. A constraint about how the organization wants to operate. These constraints are enforced by data and/or processes and are under the jurisdiction of the business. Business rules need to be supported by solution requirements.

Business Value. A concept that is unique to each organization and includes tangible and intangible elements. In business analysis, business value is considered the return, in the form of time, money, goods, or intangibles, for something exchanged.

Capability. The ability to add value or achieve objectives in an organization through a function, process, service, or other proficiency.

Competitive Analysis. A technique for obtaining and analyzing information about an organization's external environment.

Constraint. A factor that limits the options for managing a project, program, portfolio, or process. In business analysis, constraints are factors that affect the development or implementation of the solution.

Cost-Benefit Analysis. A financial analysis tool used to determine the benefits provided by a project against its costs.

Customer Journey Map. A diagram illustrating the phases that customers go through when utilizing a product and their experiences at each point in the process. It helps to provide a greater understanding about the challenges that customers face and when and how they overcome them.

Definition of Done (DoD). A series of conditions that the entire team agrees to complete before an item is considered sufficiently developed for acceptance by the business stakeholders. The DoD is often included in the acceptance criteria so it is clear to the team what exactly needs to be completed.

Deliverable. Any unique and verifiable product, result, or capability to perform a service that is produced to complete a process, phase, or project.

Disbenefit. A disbenefit is the measurable result from an outcome that is perceived as negative by one or more stakeholders. Disbenefits use activities and processes that are similar to those used in benefits management. They should be identified, categorized, quantified, and measured in the same manner as benefits.

Elicitation. The activity of drawing out information from stakeholders and other sources for the purpose of further understanding the needs of the business, addressing a problem or opportunity, and determining stakeholder preferences and conditions for the solution that will address those needs.

Empathy Map. A visualization tool that captures information about a particular type of user. Aspects of the user typically captured include what they say, think, do, and feel.

Enterprise Environmental Factors (EEFs). Conditions, not under the immediate control of the team, that influence, constrain, or direct the project, program, or portfolio.

Epic. A large user story that is too big to construct in an iteration. See also *user story*.

Facilitated Workshop. In business analysis, facilitated workshops use a structured meeting led by a skilled, neutral facilitator and a carefully selected group of stakeholders to collaborate and work toward a stated objective. Requirements workshops bring together a carefully selected group of stakeholders to collaborate, explore, and evaluate product requirements.

Feasibility Analysis. A study that produces a potential recommendation to address business needs. It examines feasibility using one or more of the following variables: operational, technology/system, cost-effectiveness, and timeliness of the potential solution.

Feature. A set of related requirements typically described by a short phrase.

Gap Analysis. A technique for understanding the gap between current capabilities and needed capabilities. Filling the gap is what comprises a solution recommendation.

Go Fever. The overall attitude of being in a hurry to complete a solution, project, or task while overlooking potential problems or mistakes.

Go/No-Go Decision. The process of determining if an initiative should continue or be stopped. This process usually involves analysis of the current state of the initiative. A "go" permits the release of the solution in whole or in part. A "no-go" either delays or disapproves the release of the solution.

Implementation Approach. A plan that outlines the steps intended to be taken to reach a solution.

Initiative. A project or action that is taken to attain an opportunity or solve a problem.

Interview. A formal or informal approach to elicit information from an individual or small group of stakeholders by asking questions and documenting the responses provided by the interviewees.

Iteration. A timeboxed cycle of development on a product or deliverable in which all of the work that is needed to deliver value is performed.

Key Performance Indicators (KPIs). Metrics defined by an organization's leadership that are used to evaluate an organization's progress toward meeting the targets or end states identified in their objectives or goals.

Level of Impact. How significantly the solution will impact the stakeholder once it is implemented.

Level of Influence. Ability to influence the product or solution requirements.

Method. A means for achieving an outcome, output, result, or project deliverable.

Model. A visual representation of information, both abstract and specific, which operates under a set of guidelines in order to efficiently arrange and convey a lot of information in an efficient manner.

Noncompliance. Failure to act or comply with a specified guideline or governance framework.

Opportunity. In business analysis, an opportunity is an uncertainty that would have a positive effect on a product or solution.

Policy. A structured pattern of actions adopted by an organization such that the organization's policy can be explained as a set of basic principles that govern the organization's conduct.

Problem. An internal or external environmental area of an organization that is causing detriment to the organization, for example, lost revenue, dissatisfied customers, delays in launching new products, or noncompliance with government regulations.

Procedure. An established method of accomplishing a consistent performance or result. A procedure typically can be described as the sequence of steps that will be used to execute a process.

Process. A systematic series of activities directed toward causing an end result such that one or more inputs will be acted upon to create one or more outputs.

Process Flow. A business analysis model that visually shows the steps taken in a process by a human user as it interacts with an implementation. A set of steps taken by a system can be shown in a similar model as a system flow.

Process Model. A visual representation of a process.

Product Roadmap. A high-level view of the features and functionality to include in a product, along with the sequence in which they will be built or delivered.

Product Scope. The features and functions that characterize a product, service, or result.

Product Team. The team that will work on a solution for a problem or opportunity.

Product Vision. An explanation of the product, its intended customers, and how needs will be met. The product vision is developed to help product teams envision what needs to be built.

Program Manager. The person authorized by the performing organization to lead the team or teams responsible for achieving program objectives.

Project Charter. A document issued by the project initiator or sponsor that formally authorizes the existence of a project and provides the project manager with the authority to apply organizational resources to project activities.

Project Management Office (PMO). A management structure that standardizes the project-related governance processes and facilitates the sharing of resources, methodologies, tools, and techniques.

Project Manager. The person assigned by the performing organization to lead the team that is responsible for achieving the project objectives.

Readiness Assessment. An assessment that occurs as the organization approaches solution deployment. It helps the organization understand the extent to which the organization is prepared for the transition and evaluates the organization's readiness to integrate and sustain the solution.

Readiness Assessment Plan. A plan developed before assessing organizational readiness that highlights the essential elements that must be in place for a successful solution transition. It should identify what will be measured, how it will be measured, and the roles and responsibilities for assessing readiness.

Regulation. A requirement imposed by a governmental body. These requirements can establish product, process, or service characteristics, including applicable administrative provisions that have government-mandated compliance.

Release. One or more components of one or more products which are intended to be put into production at the same time.

Repository. A central location for storing content.

Requirement. A condition or capability that is necessary to be present in a product, service, or result to satisfy a business need.

Risk. An uncertain event or condition that, if it occurs, has a positive or negative effect on one or more project objectives. Business analysis supports risk management processes through the identification and analysis of risks that impact business analysis activities and/or the solution.

Risk Assessment. The process of examining a program, project, or process for business-analysis-related risk.

Stakeholder. In business analysis, stakeholders are individuals, groups, or organizations that may impact, are impacted by, or have yet to be impacted by a problem or opportunity under assessment.

Standard. A guideline often established by an organization.

Technique. A defined systematic procedure employed by a human resource to perform an activity to produce a product or result or deliver a service, and that may employ one or more tools.

Tool. Something tangible, such as a template or software program, used in performing an activity to produce a product or result.

Traceability. The ability to track information across the product life cycle by establishing linkages between objects.

Tracing. See *traceability*.

Transition Plan. Defines the activities required to transition from the current to a future state.

Transition Strategy. A guiding framework for conducting activities that are needed to transition from a current state to a future state.

User Story. A one- or two-sentence description written from the viewpoint of the actor that describes a function that is needed. A user story usually takes the form of "as an <actor>, I want to <function>, so that I can <benefit>."

Value Delivery Office (VDO). A project delivery support structure that focuses on coaching teams, building agile skills and capabilities throughout the organization, and mentoring sponsors and product owners to be more effective in those roles.

Value Proposition. The value of a product or service that an organization communicates to its customers. It explains the value of the work being conducted.

Value Stream Map. A variation of process flows that can be used to locate delays, queues, or handoffs occurring in current processes.

Index